CONTEMPORARY WRITERS

General Editors
MALCOLM BRADBURY
and
CHRISTOPHER BIGSBY

JOE ORTON

JOE
ORTON

C. W. E. BIGSBY

METHUEN
LONDON AND NEW YORK

First published in 1982 by
Methuen & Co. Ltd
11 New Fetter Lane, London EC4P 4EE
Published in the USA by
Methuen & Co.
in association with Methuen, Inc.
733 Third Avenue, New York, NY 10017

© *1982 C. W. E. Bigsby*

Typeset by Rowland Phototypesetting Ltd
Printed in Great Britain by
Richard Clay (The Chaucer Press) Ltd
Bungay, Suffolk

British Library Cataloguing in Publication Data

Bigsby, C. W. E.
Joe Orton.—(Contemporary writers)
1. Orton, Joe—Criticism and interpretation
I. Title   *II. Series*
822'.914   *PR6065.R7Z/*

ISBN 0-416-31690-5

Library of Congress Cataloging in Publication Data

Bigsby, C. W. E.
Joe Orton.
(Contemporary writers)
Bibliography: p.
1. Orton, Joe—Criticism and interpretation.
I. Title.   *II. Series.*
PR6065.R7Z65   *1982*   *822'.914*   *81-22518*
ISBN 0-416-31690-5 (pbk.)

*For Ihab and
Sally Hassan*

CONTENTS

GENERAL EDITORS' PREFACE

Over the past twenty years or so, it has become clear that a decisive change has taken place in the spirit and character of contemporary writing. There now exists around us, in fiction, drama and poetry, a major achievement which belongs to our experience, our doubts and uncertainties, our ways of perceiving — an achievement stylistically radical and novel, and likely to be regarded as quite as exciting, important and innovative as that of any previous period. This is a consciousness and a confidence that has grown very slowly. In the 1950s it seemed that, somewhere amidst the dark realities of the Second World War, the great modernist impulse of the early years of this century had exhausted itself, and that the post-war arts would be arts of recessiveness, pale imitation, relative sterility. Some, indeed, doubted the ability of literature to survive the experiences of holocaust. A few major figures seemed to exist, but not a style or a direction. By the 1960s the confidence was greater, the sense of an avant-garde returned, the talents multiplied, and there was a growing hunger to define the appropriate styles, tendencies and forms of a new time. And by the 1970s it was not hard to see that we were now surrounded by a remarkable, plural, innovative generation, indeed several layers of generations, whose works represented a radical inquiry into contemporary forms and required us to read and understand — or, often, to read and *not* understand — in quite new ways. Today, as the 1980s start, that cumulative post-war achievement has acquired a degree of coherence that allows for critical response and understanding; hence the present series.

We thus start it in the conviction that the age of Beckett, Borges, Nabokov, Bellow, Pynchon, Robbe-Grillet, Golding, Murdoch, Fowles, Grass, Handke and Calvino, of Albee, Mamet, Shepard, Ionesco, Orton, Pinter and Stoppard, of Ginsberg, Lowell, Ashbery, Paz, Larkin and Hughes, and many another, is indeed an outstanding age of international creation, striking experiment, and some degree of aesthetic coherence. It is a time that has been described as 'post-modern', in the sense that it is an era consequent to modernism yet different from it, having its own distinctive preoccupations and stylistic choices. That term has its limitations, because it is apt to generate too precise definitions of the contemporary experiment, and has acquired rather too specific associations with contemporary American writing; but it does help concentrate our sense of living in a distinctive period. With the new writing has come a new criticism or rather a new critical theorem, its thrust being 'structuralist' or 'deconstructive' – a theorem that not only coexists with but has affected that writing (to the point where many of the best theorists write fictions, the best fictionalists write criticism). Again, its theory can be hermetic and enclosing, if not profoundly apocalyptic; but it points to the presence in our time of a new sense of the status of word and text, author and reader, which shapes and structures the making of modern form.

The aim of 'Contemporary Writers' is to consider some of the most important figures in this scene, looking from the standpoint of and at the achievement of the writers themselves. Its aims are eclectic, and it will follow no tight definition of the contemporary; it will function on the assumption that contemporary writing is by its nature multidirectional and elusive, since styles and directions keep constantly changing in writers who, unlike the writers of the past, are continuous, incomplete, not dead (though several of these studies will address the careers of those who, though dead, remain our contemporaries, as many of those who continue to write are manifestly not). A fair criticism of living writers must be assertive but also provisional, just as a fair sense of contemporary style must be open to that most crucial of contemporary awarenesses, that of the suddenness of change. We do not assume, then, that there is one right path to contemporary experiment, nor that a self-conscious reflexiveness, a deconstructive strategy, an art of performance or a metafictional mode is the only one of current importance. As Iris Murdoch said, 'a strong agile realism which is of course not photographic naturalism' – associated perhaps especially with British writing, but also with Latin-American and American – is also a major component of modern style.

So in this series we wish to identify major writers, some of whom are avant-garde, others who are familiar, even popular, but all of whom are in some serious sense contemporary and in some contemporary sense serious. The aim is to offer brief, lucid studies of their work which draw on modern theoretical issues but respond, as much modern criticism does not, to their distinctiveness and individual interest. We have looked for contributors who are engaged with their subjects – some of them being significant practising authors themselves, writing out of creative experience, others of whom are critics whose interest is personal as well as theoretical. Each volume will provide a thorough account of the author's work so far, a solid bibliography, a personal judgement – and, we hope, an enlarged understanding of writers who are important, not only because of the individual force of their work, but because they are ours in ways no past writer could really be.

Norwich, England, 1981

MALCOLM BRADBURY
CHRISTOPHER BIGSBY

ACKNOWLEDGEMENTS

To anyone writing about Joe Orton, John Lahr's biography *Prick Up Your Ears* (1978) is a central text. I should like to acknowledge my debt to it here.

The author and publishers wish to thank Eyre Methuen Ltd for permission to reproduce copyright material from *Joe Orton: The Complete Plays* (1976).

A NOTE ON THE TEXTS

Page references to Orton's plays are from *Joe Orton: The Complete Plays* (London: Eyre Methuen, 1976).

1

JOE ORTON AND THE DEATH OF CHARACTER

Is the world mad?
I'm not paid to quarrel with accepted facts.   (Joe Orton)

Man is least himself when he talks in his own person. Give
him a mask and he will tell you the truth.   (Oscar Wilde)

In 1965 the American novelist John Hawkes offered an
account of his own artistic principles which has increasingly
come to seem a classic summary of that experimental stance
known as post-modernism: 'I began to write fiction', he
observed, 'on the assumption that the true enemies of the novel
were plot, character, setting and theme, and having once
abandoned these familiar ways of thinking about fiction, totality of vision or structure was really all that remained.'[1] Certainly recent serious discussion of contemporary fiction has
tended to concentrate on the deconstruction of such recognizable conventions of realism. It has stressed fictiveness and the
relativity of perception; it has emphasized the parodic element
in art, the decreation of character and narrative, the contingency of experience and the text, the authoritarian nature of
the social world and the imagination alike, the loss of the self
and the dissolution of social and moral models. Old paradigms
of experience and form no longer seem to satisfy.

As early as 1957 Alain Robbe-Grillet was writing that 'The
novel that contains characters belongs well and truly to the
past, it was peculiar to an age.' Equally suspect was plot,
because it implied a specious rationalism, an illusion of natural
order with metaphysical and social implications, 'whose development corresponds to the assumption of power by the
middle classes', and which 'aimed at imposing the magic of a
stable universe, coherent, continuous, univocal, and wholly

13

decipherable'.[2] And in the modern novel – the fiction of, say, Thomas Pynchon, Peter Handke, Jerzy Kosinski, John Hawkes and Robbe-Grillet himself – some essential absurdity, part social and historical, part metaphysical, has indeed created an evident instability. Perhaps for historical reasons (the literal reduction of the human body to inanimate object or ash in the battles, the firestorms and the concentration camps of the Second World War has been a dominant image or motivating fact in much modern writing, invoked by those, like Vonnegut, Hawkes and Robbe-Grillet, who experienced it directly, as well as by those, like Pynchon, who did not) but also because of changing theories of the status of the subject and of the word, notions of a clearly defined place for the human figure, of the integrity of the human form, of an implied contract between individual and society or men and things, no longer seem self-evident constituents of art.

These changes do have their equivalents in theatre, but these tend to attract less attention, to command less critical engagement. Perhaps the reason for this is a function less of simple critical disregard than of the nature of theatre itself. In an age of anxiety the theatre still appears to offer a certain reassurance. Not only does it present an ordered world in which contingency is tamed, forced back behind the bars of time and place, contained within this 'wooden O'; it also appears to affirm the substantiality of the human person. Unlike the purely literary genres, it offers the living presence of the actor and of the audience who come together in at least the semblance of community. The two-dimensionality of the printed word becomes the three-dimensionality of the enacted word; fictive gestures become plastic forms. So the person, consciously evacuated from so much contemporary fiction, is seemingly restored, quite literally, to centre stage, and hence theatre would appear to reaffirm at least some of the old models of character and behaviour.

Yet absurdity has plainly not been absent from our stage: the drama of Ionesco and Beckett has been as conscious of these deconstructions as has the novel. Their plays may take the human figure, but they disassemble and distance it, display it in a world of deforming absurdities. And increasingly, in exploring the paradoxes equally present in other post-modern forms,

14

theatre has turned to examine its own theatricality.

Indeed, in many ways the theatre constitutes a naturally reflexive setting, one that might seem more ideally suited to the exploration of many post-modern concerns than is the novel. The fictive quality of drama is, after all, inescapable; as with crustacea, its skeleton is always on the outside.

The circumstances of theatre inevitably create a distance, a perspective, that is absent from the novel. It constantly confesses to its fictiveness as even the film, for example, does not. The imaginative process is externalized, acted out, mediated, by actors, directors and the *mise-en-scène*. Theatre stresses the relativity of art, language, character and text (in that these are constantly modified by performance); the action, for the most part, takes place on an obvious stage. With films, the screen vanishes as soon as the image appears and so, to a degree, does the audience, since with no possibility of feedback it has little role to play. With theatre, the stage remains clearly in evidence and the audience recognizes its own role in the events. The film maker can choose to foreground technique, as Godard does. But with theatre that foregrounding is inescapable. The only option is to emphasize it or work to diminish it. To a degree, therefore, the subject of theatre is always in a sense theatre itself. The very word 'play' emphasizes the game element of drama, the pretence; it implies almost a parodic element, at its most intense in the form of farce – the hyper-theatrical form which by its very nature emphasizes and parodies the component parts of theatrical experience.

Meanwhile the role playing of the actors offers a constant reminder of the role playing of the audience, whose very status *as* an audience is adopted only for the duration of the performance. And there is, of course, an inevitable parallel between the role playing of the theatre and that of what with decreasing confidence we choose to call 'real life'. During the 1960s, indeed, the theatre came to be seen as an appropriate metaphor of human relationships (as it was, admittedly, for Shakespeare) for sociologists like Erving Goffman, for psycho-historians like Norman O. Brown, for psychologists like R. D. Laing, for psychotherapists and social workers. Literary criticism began to talk of a performing self (Richard Poirier): Robert Brustein published a book entitled *Revolution as Theatre* (1971); John

Lahr produced *Life Show* (1973), with the subtitle *How to See Life in Theatre and Theatre in Life*. Increasingly the idea of identity as the interleaving of roles, a structure of performance, was appropriated by the social sciences and then reabsorbed back into the theatre, whose theorists in turn began to investigate the writings of anthropologists, neo-Freudians, gestalt psychologists and communication theorists. And, in this re-examination of theatricality, the fictionalizing process moved to the forefront.

And yet, of course, as suggested above, countering the strongly foregrounded fictiveness of theatre is an apparently ineluctable three-dimensionality. An art of surfaces is difficult when one is confronted with the living embodiments of the dramatist's imagination, who by their presence seem to reinstate a sense of character that the writer may feel to have been expelled by history or the simple ironies of existence. In conventional textbooks on drama, character usually warrants a chapter to itself. It is offered as definitional of a genre that, whatever its mystical or epic origins, has become a primary expression of bourgeois individualism. Theatre, in its modern form, is seen as an art in which characters are the agents of empathetic response, figures by means of which we are drawn to acknowledge the analogical powers of theatre.

So strong is this element that Bertolt Brecht set himself specifically to disrupt it, to reduce character to ideological marker, to an element in his dialectics. It proved remarkably resistant. But in the post-war world character, no less than language and plot, has come under increasing pressure, and the writer who wishes to confess to this pressure, who wishes to assert the reductive nature of the human experience, the displacement of the subject, has resorted to a number of strategies. One has been to parody the apparent substantiality of the actor by treating the body as an object — as Beckett does in *Not I*, Ionesco does in *Amédée, or How to Get Rid of It*, Albee does in *Quotations from Chairman Mao Tse-Tung* and Jean-Claude van Itallie does in *Motel*. Another has been to remove it entirely, as in Albee's *Box* or Paul Foster's *Balls*. But the deconstruction of character has always been a standard strategy of farce; and though there is, perhaps consequently, a strong farce element in absurdist drama, relatively little attention has been paid to farce itself as potentially a principal mechanism of the post-modernist impulse, or to the high priest of farce in the mid-sixties, Joe Orton. He, after all, was a man whose life and death, no less than his art, exemplified a distrust of those moral, social and psychological solidities that the theatre had once apparently accepted as its legitimate concern and defining limits; a man for whom art was model rather than analogue, for whom ethics and metaphysics deferred to aesthetics and for whom the self was the supreme fiction.

Farce has always been concerned with the elimination of character, with the creation of an almost hysterical intensity in which character is flung off by the sheer centrifugal force of language and action. But it was Orton's achievement to give farce a new meaning, to make it something more than the coy trysting with disorder it had once been. For Orton, farce became both an expression of anarchy and its only antidote. In his plays, role playing is not a series of false surfaces concealing a real self; it is the total meaning or unmeaning of protagonists who survive by refusing all substance. Where Hawkes, in rejecting plot, character, setting and theme, had clung on to 'verbal and psychological coherence', Orton dispensed even with these.

And because the theatre is about presence – the presence of the actor and of the audience – it is well adapted to enforce a sense of significant absence. The absence of Godot, for example, is in a sense the primary fact of Beckett's play. Likewise the absence of a third dimension to character underlines a critical collapse in the world of Orton's plays, as does the parallel absence of a moral perspective and a language, dense with meaning, generated by a series of unique sensibilities. Where the modernist writer had seen in art itself some final recourse in the face of social and moral collapse, a separate world in which coherence, function and grace could survive, Orton permitted no such consolation. The process of his plays is one of unmaking rather than unmasking. His work is as much a critique of theatre (though especially of bad theatre) as it is a comment on the apparent substantialities of the world at whose hands he suffered. If his work, in common with that of Beckett, rejects what Fausto Maijstral in Thomas Pynchon's *V.* calls the fiction of continuity, the fiction of cause and effect, the fiction of a humanized history endowed with reason, it also casts doubt on its own status. It is not so much an art of mimetic gestures copying a secure reality, but rather an art of entropic enactments, rendering his sense of the depleting energy of the human machine. It constitutes a series of confessions of fictional fragility, denials of coherence and meaning. Despite their structured form, their 'framing' of experience, his plays are self-destructing mechanisms, and their subject is thus as much themselves – the absurd pitching of the pattern-forming power of art against the disorder of experience – as it is a comment on that disorder itself. Drama as metadrama.

For Jasper Johns, flatness was a quality specific to painting; but, like Johns, Warhol, Oldenberg and Lichtenstein, Orton also presents a world in which the surface is the reality, a post-moral world. His work simultaneously parodies and celebrates. And like Warhol he devised a public persona as fragile and as evanescent as that of his characters. (The very word 'person', after all, was a theatrical term, deriving from the Greek word for the mask used in classical drama. It was in origin, therefore, not a substantial unifying reality. It was multiform, the many voices of drama providing the playwright with a multiple identity. Orton merely extended this logic to his own life.) For Orton, the power of character is broken primarily because it no longer has authority in the anxious world outside art. Not himself allowed the autonomy necessary to identity, he retreated into a mannered role playing which he then proposed as a model for social action. He played his roles with total conviction and was very much his own creation. He falsely declared himself to be an orphan, as did his homosexual lover; he changed his first name, as did Ronald Firbank, one of his literary models. He was contemptuous of the society that simultaneously despised him as a person and exalted him as a celebrity. He was, in all, very much a figure of the sixties. He lived an intense, brittle existence, was fascinated by the violent underside of society and the homosexual world of style, disguise and illegality, and celebrated his own conspicuous nonconformity as an image of the times. His disregard for the symbols of public order, his unashamed concern with sexuality and his disruptive wit made him that rarity in English writing, a genuine subversive, a social and literary anarchist.

His public career lasted a bare three years, and his total dramatic output comprised only three full-length plays, a screenplay and four one-act works, three of which were originally written for television. None the less, his impact on the English theatre was considerable, and his reputation became international. Ironically, it was this very success which led to his death at the age of thirty-four. For, on 9 August 1967, his lover, overcome by feelings of his own inadequacy in the face of Orton's achievements, took a hammer and bludgeoned him to death before himself committing suicide. Their deaths were as much of a scandal as their lives had been, the violent assault on Orton's nude body providing an ironic reflection of the process of many of the plays that he left behind as an extraordinary and innovative contribution to theatre. Not merely life, it seemed, but also death followed art. Today he remains our contemporary, as many who survived him are patently not.

*

John Kingsley Orton was born in Leicester in 1933. He left school at the age of sixteen and went to the Royal Academy of Dramatic Art in 1950, graduating in 1953. His acting career lasted only some six months, after which he settled down with his homosexual companion Kenneth Halliwell, to write novels. With such revealing titles as *The Last Days of Sodom*, *Priapus in the Shrubbery* and *The Mechanical Womb*, these were never published, though a Nathanael-West-like fantasy, which Orton wrote on his own in 1961, *The Vision of Gombold Proval*, did appear four years after his death under the title *Head to Toe*. Their joint aspirations outstripped their joint talents, and their subversive energies were accordingly channelled in another direction. In 1962 both Halliwell and Orton were arrested, charged with stealing and defacing books (they were alleged to have stolen 83 books and 1653 plates). Among other enormities, they had pasted the picture of a naked tattooed man over a photograph of the Poet Laureate John Betjeman – an extreme form of literary criticism which, warranted or not, was not appreciated by the guardians of Islington Public Library. Unbelievably, for this anti-art gesture they were both sentenced to six months in prison.

It was a crucial event, for while Halliwell was shocked into an attempted suicide Orton looked on the experience as a revelation of the hypocrisy and inhumanity of society. As a homosexual he already felt menaced by authority, but he now saw at first hand its ability to humiliate and injure and as a consequence felt relieved of any responsibility to it. As he explained: 'Before I had been vaguely conscious of something rotting somewhere; prison crystallised this. The old whore society really lifted up her skirts and the stench was pretty foul.'[3]

In many ways Orton's mere existence was regarded as an affront by society. His particular kind of sexuality was legally outlawed, his anarchic humour seen as a challenge by petty officialdom (the campaign conducted by the Islington librarian to catch him 'improving' the dust-jackets of library books was conducted with such vigour and pride that it was written up for the *Library Association Record*). But his battle with society could plainly not be won by direct assault, by simple action. His principal weapon was to be his writing, and that is acknowledged plainly enough in *Head to Toe*, the novel he wrote before his arrest: 'Gombold realised that the tactics which he had been using had proved useless. Words were more effective than actions; in the right hands verbs and nouns could create panic.' Thus Gombold, a human parasite who finds himself suddenly and inexplicably stranded on the huge body of an anonymous giant, buys a dictionary, as Orton himself assiduously wrote out lists of words and phrases in order to perfect his style. At the time of writing Orton saw himself as a putative novelist, but already his subversive logic was beginning to lead him towards the theatre, for reasons that are implicit in Gombold's own developing linguistic strategy:

The blast of a long sentence was curiously local, and a lot of shorter sentences seemed better. And then there was the problem of gathering enough of the enemy together in order that they might listen. He started wondering where and how he could hit the enemy most. . . . He thought of a book. But there was no use. It would vibrate the structure but not enough. To be destructive, words had to be irrefutable. And then the book might not be read. He was aware that words and sentences often buried themselves into readers' minds before exploding and then went off harmlessly. Print was less effective than the spoken word because the blast was greater; eyes could ignore, slide past, dangerous verbs or nouns. But if you could lock the enemy into a room somewhere and fire the sentence at them you could get a sort of seismic disturbance . . .[4]

For Orton, the man who had lingered in the Islington and Hampstead libraries in order to see the impact of his subversive work on those who picked up his doctored books, it was essential to see the effect of his work. The theatre was the logical answer. Here he could indeed lock the enemy into a room and fire sentences at them; here the spoken word could do its destructive work.

Language became a weapon for Orton no less than for Gombold – who 'studied the chemistry and behaviour of words, phrase design, the forging, casting and milling, the theories of paraphrase and periphrase, the fusing and the airing.' Just as Orton was to study the work of Congreve and Wycherley, of Wilde and Feydeau, so, in a library, Gombold 'unearthed accounts of the damage words had done in the past. His figures showed that when a particularly dangerous collection of words exploded the shock waves were capable of killing centuries afterwards' (p. 149).

For Orton, his was a decaying society. Its values were outmoded, its art pusillanimous, and yet no one seemed willing to draw the inevitable conclusions. Osborne's image of Britain as a decaying music hall presided over by a seedy comedian, in *The Entertainer*, was too gentle, too sentimental. For Orton, the appropriate image for the body politic was that of a giant decaying corpse inhabited by human lice desperately denying the evidence of putrefaction. 'The prospect of living on a corpse did not affect many people,' he insists.

Indeed there were those who maintained the giant was not dead. Presented with the rotting flesh and the presence of maggots where once had been pleasant acres, they spoke in terms of temporary phenomena. 'I expect it'll blow over,' said a woman pushing a pram. (p. 157)

Head to Toe is a crucial text. It is not hard to see the figure of Gombold, trapped in a world of sexual ambiguity and praying for 'the ability to rage correctly', as an image of Orton himself. For him, prison had been a crucial experience. So, ironically, it had proved for Gombold, though his fictional imprisonment actually predated Orton's:

> Gombold, the prisoner, imprisoning reason, experienced an opening of windows, a smashing of barriers, and a cleansing . . . wheels, springs and coils of sense and nonsense. He had succeeded in breaking down the walls so that his experience recorded clear and true, in its totality, was not a single unit, but many separate units, melting and fusing into a vision. (p. 61)

This is akin to the vision that Hawkes has pursued, and it gives the unity to Orton's work. For he, like his fictional protagonist, set out to imprison reason; he, too, believed that 'By use of images it might be possible to extract from fantasy a kind of reality' (p. 60). And that reality was defined by his settings (prison cells, brothels, psychiatrists' offices) and by those who inhabit those settings (undertakers, abortionists, bent policemen, sexual anarchists). His characters are abused and used by one another and by experience: they are victims. His world is one in which violation is a central trope – the final violation being death – and violence provides the constant environment.

The mood of Orton's theatre is precisely that invoked by Nathanael West in *The Dream Life of Balso Snell*, on which he surely based *Head to Toe*, and gives him a link with surrealist origins. For in that novel (in which the protagonist climbs inside a giant Trojan horse – a scene repeated in Orton's novel) a character describes his ambition to create a drama that will simultaneously satisfy and mock the pretensions of those who wish to congratulate themselves on their sophistication:

> In this play I shall take my beloved patrons into my confidence and flatter their difference from other theatre-goers. I shall congratulate them on their good taste in preferring Art to animal acts. Then, suddenly, in the midst of some very witty dialogue, the entire cast will walk to the footlights and shout Chekhov's advice: 'It would be more profitable for the farmer to raise rats for the granary than for the bourgeois to nourish the artist, who must always be occupied with undermining institutions.' In case the audience should mis-

understand and align itself on the side of the artist, the ceiling of the theatre will be made to open and cover the occupants with tons of loose excrement. After the deluge, if they so desire, the patrons of my art can gather in the customary charming groups and discuss the play.[5]

This is exactly the attitude of Orton, whose defences against criticism were as well prepared as those of the Dadaists, but who was equally aware of the capacity of critics and society to absorb the anarchic gesture. It was Marcel Duchamp, after all, who had complained that 'I threw the bottle rack and the urinal in their faces for a challenge and now they admire them for their aesthetic beauty.'[6]

Throughout his brief career he maintained a wry detachment not only from the social world but also from his own art. He was scrupulous in his attention to the details of craft, but undeceived by the mythologizing of art as an act of transcendence. For him it was a provocation, an act of revenge, a deliberate flouting of authority and flaunting of his own exhibitionist tendencies. It was designed to negate the conventional assurances of art and to corrode the link between that art and the assumptions of liberal humanism. Where, through its emphasis on the social and the psychological, liberal art offered a rational model of history and personal experience, he chose to stress the arbitrary, the irrational. Where it presented an image of a complexly motivated self in negotiation with a publicly verifiable reality, he presented a series of caricatures who exist in a self-evidently theatricalized world. Where it implied the possibility of social and moral order, the persistence of meaning, he dramatized an anarchic world, irrational, violent and self-consuming.

2

THE EARLY PLAYS

In many ways Orton's work falls into three clearly distinguishable periods. His first plays, *The Ruffian on the Stair* (radio version 1964; stage version 1966) and *Entertaining Mr Sloane* (1964), both heavily influenced by Pinter, are essentially absurdist: black comedies turning on the ironies that emerge from the collision between human aspirations and an implacable universe. These were followed by the more directly satirical *The Good and Faithful Servant* (written 1964; televised 1967), while this, in turn, was followed by the anarchic farces, *Loot* (written 1964; staged 1966), *The Erpingham Camp* (written 1965; televised 1966; staged 1967), *Funeral Games* (written 1966; televised 1968) and *What the Butler Saw* (written 1967; staged 1969). It was a development that took just three years.

The Ruffian on the Stair was Orton's first play. According to Martin Esslin, then head of radio drama at the BBC, it arrived in 1963 in a brown envelope marked 'H. M. Prisons'. Written for the radio, it was finally broadcast only after the première of his second play, *Entertaining Mr Sloane*, a work it closely resembles. Subsequently revised, it appeared on the stage in August 1966.

The resemblance between *The Ruffian on the Stair* and Pinter's *The Room* or *The Dumb Waiter* is too striking for comfort. Joyce, an ex-prostitute, lives with a hired killer called Mike. When he is out meeting his contact in the men's toilet at King's Cross Station (a typical Orton touch, with its deliberate reference to a sexuality otherwise ruthlessly censored from the radio version but reinstated in the version prepared for the stage), a third person, Wilson, arrives. As we gather from the brief verse by W. E. Henley which prefaces the play –

> Madame Life's a piece in bloom,
> Death goes dogging everywhere:
> She's the tenant of the room,
> He's the ruffian on the stair.

– he serves much the same function as the blind Negro in *The Room*. Both are images of death desperately resisted by those intent on perpetuating their comfortable, if ultimately meaningless, existence. Wilson tries to insinuate his way into the room, a room that functions, in a manner familiar from many of Pinter's early plays, as a protection against external threat. His assault precipitates a decidedly Pinteresque dialogue:

WILSON (*smiling*). I've come about the room
JOYCE. I'm afraid there's been a mistake. I've nothing to do with allotting rooms. Make your enquiries elsewhere.
WILSON. I'm not coloured. I was brought up in the Home Counties.
JOYCE. That doesn't ring a bell with me, I'm afraid.
WILSON. Is that the room?
JOYCE. That's my room.
WILSON. I couldn't share. What rent are you asking?
JOYCE. I'm not asking any.
WILSON. I don't want charity. I'd pay for my room.
JOYCE. You must have come to the wrong door. I'm sorry you've been troubled. (p. 33)

The similarity between this and an exchange in *The Room* is obvious and even embarrassing.

MRS SANDS. . . . we'd heard they'd got a room to let here, so we thought we'd come along and have a look . . .
ROSE. You won't find any rooms vacant in this house.
MR SANDS. Why not?
ROSE. Mr Kidd told me. He told me.
MR SANDS. Mr Kidd?
ROSE. He told me he was full up.

25

MR SANDS. The man in the basement said there was one. One room. Number seven he said.

Pause.

ROSE. That's this room.

MR SANDS. We'd better go and get hold of the landlord.

MRS SANDS (*rising*). Well, thank you for the warm-up, Mrs Hudd. I feel better now.

ROSE. This room is occupied.[7]

Like Pinter, Orton is concerned with underscoring the emotional and metaphysical void that he sees as lying beneath the surface of existence. Familiar settings are invested with a sense of menace. The surface realism is fractured by an external threat which exposes an internal insufficiency. *The Ruffian on the Stair* is set in 'a kitchen/living room with a bedroom alcove' and *Entertaining Mr Sloane* in 'a room' in a house situated in the middle of a rubbish dump. The cramped setting is an image of characters who are themselves effectively trapped in the narrow range of their own possibilities. But it is not a refuge that offers any protection. Once the familiar territory is breached, they are exposed, vulnerable, driven back on to resources they do not possess. Only vaguely conscious of a sense of pain and loss (in the former play) or not even aware of the existence of such emotions (in the latter), they happily embrace a vacuous routine, compounding the absurdity of their situation by their blithe insensitivity.

Unlike Edward Albee's much misunderstood play, *The Zoo Story*, *The Ruffian on the Stair* is concerned with the efforts of one character to fool another into collaborating in his own suicide. Wilson's brother has been murdered by Mike. Genuinely dismayed at the loss of a brother who was also a homosexual companion, Wilson provokes Mike into shooting him. But where Albee's play is a direct plea for human communication, for the renewal of a love destroyed or sentimentalized by contemporary society, Orton's is a demonstration of the arbitrary power of primary instincts. Where Jerry's death, in Albee's play, is a sacrifice to demonstrate the need for human commitment, Wilson's is a pointless suicide which has no effect on those who survive it. In this world the word 'sacrifice' would have no meaning at all.

Orton's first play seemed in some sense counterfeit. The dominant influence of Pinter was so strong, indeed, that he felt obliged to delete some of the more obvious borrowings when he prepared it for the stage and to insist that 'The play mustn't be presented as an example of the now outdated "mystery" school – *vide* early Pinter' (p. 17). But there was some legitimacy in such a remark, for already he was inclined to resist the implications of metaphysics. Like Robbe-Grillet, he reacted against literary speliology – the assumption that art works by concealment, with the text merely hiding a subtext which is the real repository of meaning. Besides a predilection for mischievous innuendo, he was already committed to exposure as a method, inclined to realistic production values, more committed to the pace of farce than to what he regarded as the portentous mystifications of Pinter. 'The play', he insisted, 'must be directed without long significant pauses. Any pauses must be natural. Pace, pace, pace as well' (p. 17). Such mystery as exists derives less from the unexplained than from emotions that cannot be fully articulated – a problem not without its relevance to Orton. Indeed, if anything, the weakness of the play lies in a sentimentality not entirely neutralized by a mannered language. The loneliness that drives both male protagonists escapes the ironic treatment of their character and actions. Where later he would rigorously deny his characters any emotional dimension, making them no more than the embodiments of biological drives, here he compromises, opting for absurdist melodrama rather than absurdist farce.

Orton's early characters, like Pinter's, seem to inhabit a social and moral no man's land between the working class and the lower middle class to which they aspire; they are not quite at home in either. They reveal a severely limited emotional range which is reflected in a similarly restricted linguistic competence. Their pretensions to urbanity and their language, curiously inappropriate as it is to their situation, reflect a disruption between the apparent reality of their circumstances and their perception of that reality – a disruption that has implications beyond the social. The characters are mocked by the contrast between the studied, though seldom wholly correct, formality of their language and the substance of their lives. Thus the pathos of Pinter's caretaker, a personality constantly on the verge of disintegration, derives in part from the disjunction between his language and his immediate situation. His talk of 'references' being held at Sidcup, his desperate attempt to tune into the technical language of the interior decorator, deliberately invoked by Mick as a means to ridicule him, underline his incapacity to function in the world in which he finds himself. Likewise, when the similarly named Mike, in *The Ruffian on the Stair*, enquires of his ex-prostitute lover whether she has 'allowed another man to be intimate' with her and bewails the fact that 'the morals of Nineveh were hardly so lax', we are clearly moving in a world in which reality cannot be adequately described or controlled by language — or, alternatively, in which language stands as a symbol of the kind of ordered and socially secure world which the individual would wish to occupy but cannot locate or inhabit. It is not just evidence of bourgeois pretensions, a bid for linguistic upward mobility. The secondhand expressions they use serve to underscore the degree to which they are the products of language rather than its master.

The clichés in which his characters perpetually speak imply a language drained of content. He derives his linguistic leverage from this juxtaposition of words to setting and character, both being voided of content. It is as though language were an almost dead battery he has stumbled on, able to generate only the minimum of power. It is a language marked by discontinuities, non sequiturs, incongruities. Conversations seem never to involve real exchanges. His characters are curiously autistic, incapable of communicating feeling or meaning with any conviction.

The gulf between words and action in Beckett is a measure of the individual's inability to control his circumstances. The famous contradiction between Vladimir's (and, later, Estragon's) statement 'let's go' and the subsequent stage direction indicating that 'They do not move' is a paradigm of human impotence. So it is here. For both Pinter and Orton it also signifies a willed self-deception, an attempt to remake reality with language. But, more fundamentally, the world that Orton describes is spiritually attenuated — a place in which a debilitated language reflects a parallel collapse of all other human values and civilizing qualities. It is a world that can accept violence and even murder as of no more significance than the accidental death of a pet goldfish. It is a life in which the primary facts are sex and violence.

This is certainly true of *Entertaining Mr Sloane*, in which Kath, a forty-one-year-old nymphomaniac who has had a child by her homosexual brother's boyfriend, is made pregnant by her new lodger, Mr Sloane. Like Mike, in Orton's first play, he is a youthful murderer. We learn that he had murdered her brother's employer (a pornographic photographer) two years before and we now see him murder her father, kicking him to death with cool indifference. The play ends as Kath and her brother Ed decide to make use of Sloane's sexual proclivities on a co-operative basis, each gaining use of his services for six months.

Like his first play, *Entertaining Mr Sloane* owes a great deal to Pinter. Sloane himself is close kin to Stanley in Pinter's *The Birthday Party*. Both are lodgers pursued by repulsive middle-aged landladies. Both move from being contemptuously dominant to being the pliant victims of others. Both plays end on an ironic note as the mindless pattern of existence reasserts itself and the disturbing revelations of insecurity and violence go disregarded. *The Birthday Party* ends with Meg congratulating herself on her nonexistent charm as Stanley is driven away in a state of shock; Orton's second play ends with Kath happily sucking on a boiled sweet as her father lies dead in a room above. Indeed, in many respects Meg and Kath are simply two versions of the same character. Both display a grotesque mixture of motherly love and lust; both are the uncomprehending victims of impulses and circumstances which they fail to perceive in any adequate way, animated as they are only by a grotesque sexual urge.

The object of that urge, here, as in *The Ruffian on the Stair*, is himself a grotesque, for Sloane is in truth an idle, violent psychopath. Like Carson McCullers, in *The Ballad of the Sad Café*, Orton seems intent, at this stage, on underscoring the absurd determinism that directs human relationships — the destructive centrality of a sexual impulse that transforms those relationships into a battle for survival, an exploitative arena. And sex is central to his work in a way that it is not, to the same degree, to Pinter's. For Orton, in his early works, it is at the heart of events, maiming, infantilizing, brutalizing. All other activity, with the exception of a sexually derived violence, is relegated to the wings. The grotesque power of the sexual drive is presented not only as an image of alienation but as, in some degree, its cause. The social world is merely cover for an aggression that projects tensions on to a public screen. For Pinter, sex is not the source of the menace he dramatizes so effectively. It is only one form of human vulnerability, since to desire is to become a victim, to reveal a weakness. The battle for dominance may assume a sexual dimension in *The Homecoming* or in *Old Times*, but this in turn is a single aspect of a struggle that is inherent in human nature.

Orton obviously owes a great deal to the absurdists. The cramped setting, the marginal characters conversing in clichés, the irrelevance of social referents, the painful gulf between aspiration and fulfilment, between language and reality, are familiar enough. For Orton, as for Beckett, character is no longer rooted in an identifiable moral world, if it ever was. Detached from history and geography, unable to conceive of transcendent values, his characters remain unchanged in their essential nature. Both writers deny the significance of shifting social pressures and see the parameters of moral and social force as being of no consequence. The demeaning reality of biology constitutes the only metaphysics. In Orton's work liberal principles become no more than a cover for sexual assault. When Ed is accused of lacking principles, his affronted response is deflatingly double-edged: 'You really have hurt me now. . . . Why do thinking men everywhere show young boys the straight and narrow. . . . Support the Scout-movement? Principles, boy, bleeding principles' (p. 134). Sloane's knowing reply underscores the collapse alike of a moral view and of the language that supported it: 'A couple of years ago I met a man similar to yourself. Same outlook on life. . . . He was an expert on the adolescent male boy. . . . During the course of one magical night he talked to me of his principles' (p. 135).

In this world there is no structure, and the dominating sexual image is itself indicative of a fundamental dissonance. It is not only a world of grotesque mismatches, but one in which the incestuous relationship is the norm. It is hinted that Sloane may be Kath's illegitimate child; in *The Ruffian on the Stair* Wilson has been having a homosexual relationship with his brother, a relationship described, by Orton, as a sexual perversion for which not even the Irish have a name. For Freud incest was an image of anarchy, and in all of Orton's work this anarchy dominates – either, in his early work, as a natural product of absurdity or, in his later work, as a redemptive volatility.

The world of *The Ruffian on the Stair* and *Entertaining Mr Sloane* is one of moral and linguistic incoherences. His characters are in control of neither their language nor their actions. Sexual impulses are the primary motor forces of their behaviour, but they each inhabit separate worlds. They are the objects of humour rather than its conscious generators. Thus the humour frequently derives from innuendoes lost on the characters, from an absurdly inappropriate register or vocabulary to which they themselves are insensitive. They are purely theatrical figures – a status to which the text itself confesses. So, in *Entertaining Mr Sloane*, Kath asks Sloane to 'Kiss my hand, dear, in the manner of the theatre' (p. 143), while Ed accuses her of giving a 'cruel performance'. Much of the dialogue in the play consists of short sentences, quick-fire exchanges reminiscent of the music hall, which is plainly one of Orton's models. And as he chose to stress the theatricality of his characters, so he suppressed the sentimentality of his first play, opting for a world in which the density of character and the complexity of social reality are denied. The chief threat now becomes for him, as it did for Albee in *The American Dream* or Pynchon in *V.*, the pull of the inanimate, as his figures are slowly dismantled, invaded by the mechanical, from Kath's false teeth ('My teeth, since you mentioned the subject, Mr Sloane, are in the kitchen in Stergene', p. 99) to Buchanan's artificial arm, in *The Good and Faithful Servant* ('I like to know where I am in relation to the number of limbs a man has,' objects his wife-to-be), and the corpse's glass eye in *Loot*. Indeed, Orton's plays are as littered with corpses as revenge tragedy, a genre whose fascination with death, moral anarchy and insanity attracted Orton to the extent that he used a passage from *The Revenger's Tragedy* as epigraph to his last play.

The violation of conventional modes and a refusal to accept the logic of narrative or character development are central strategies. Like Eliot and Pinter before him, Orton relies on the theatre's conventional function as a source of reassurance and entertainment for his subversive effects, making conscious use of the conventions he was intent on undermining. Thus Eliot's metaphysics relied specifically on the prosaic realism, the model of an ordered and fundamentally unserious existence, of the drawing-room drama; Pinter relied both on this and on the simple naturalism of the new English social drama (Wesker's and Delaney's working-class kitchens), as on a longer tradition of British theatre. Assumptions about the nature of the genre, the significance of a familiar *mise-en-scène*, the relationship between character and language, the existence and reality of a moral world, were essential to work whose effect depended precisely on its refusal to confirm those assumptions: so, in a sense, the ideal audience for such plays was not one fully adjusted to the experimentalism of the art theatre but rather the middle-brow adherents of the West End. And, interestingly enough, this is where Pinter and Orton's first plays were performed.

Orton's antitheatre is designed to explode the form in much the same way as Nathalie Sarraute's novels. As Jean-Paul Sartre explained, in a preface to her *Portrait d'un inconnu*:

> Antinovels preserve the appearance and the contours of the novel. . . . But that is in order to deceive [or disappoint] the better; it is a matter of making the novel fall into dispute with itself, of destroying it beneath our eyes at the same time as it seems to be building it up.[8]

When Orton insisted, of the stage version of *Ruffian on the Stair*, that 'Everything is as clear as the most reactionary *Telegraph* reader could wish. There is a beginning, a middle and an end,' he acknowledged a similar tactic, taunting his audience with its need for a reassuring order in art to match its desire for a disciplined and ordered society. Yet the structuring is deceptive. Thus Orton's elaborate plots do not imply that he is intent on imposing order on a recalcitrant reality, or creating comfortable fictions to oppose to disturbing notions of flux. His complex plots are in fact parodies of form, ironic comments on the failure of nerve exemplified by sub-genres such as the conventional farce and the whodunit. Where these permit a provisional dislocation of the pattern, they do so merely to reconstruct it.

Orton's plays almost invariably conclude with a return to consonance which can be nothing but ironic. *Funeral Games* closes with the police getting their man (the wrong man, as it turns out), as the murderer remarks, 'Do not weep. Everything works out in accordance with the divine Will'; while *The Good and Faithful Servant* ends with the announcement of the protagonist's death to the accompaniment of 'On the Sunny Side of the Street'. The same reductive irony operates in the grotesquely inappropriate iconography and rhetoric that concludes *The Erpingham Camp*, in which, as the stage direction indicates, 'the body of Erpingham is left alone in the moonlight with the red balloons and dying flames in a blaze from the distant stained glass. A great choir is heard singing "The Holy City".' Thus, from the final line of *Loot*, 'We must keep up appearances', to the bizarre concluding remarks of *What the Butler Saw*, 'I'm glad you don't despise tradition. Let us put our clothes on and face the world. *They pick up their clothes and, weary, bleeding, drugged and drunk, climb the rope ladder into the blazing light*', Orton seems intent on simultaneously satisfying and ridiculing the demands of a form that derives its effect from the re-establishment of rationality and structure after a simulated flirting with formlessness. While justice and morality seem to be victorious, in fact they have been profoundly subverted. Taken seriously, the final stage direction of *The Ruffian on the Stair* seems to indicate the reality of compassion and hope, the possibility of restoring a relationship through suffering: '*Joyce is too heartbroken to answer. She buries her face in Mike's shoulder. He holds her close.*' In fact, Mike is a hired killer who needs Joyce's evidence to substantiate his alibi, while Joyce is upset not as a result of the man she has just seen killed but because her goldfish have been destroyed by a stray bullet.

Orton's characters are deliberately flattened, deprived of the supposed depth of realism: they are simple caricatures, reduced to the two-dimensionality of a painting. Jackson Pollock once observed that 'There was a reviewer a while back who wrote that my pictures didn't have any beginning middle or end. He didn't mean it as a compliment, but it was. It was a fine compliment'.[9] By contrast, Orton chooses less to destroy such a structure from without, by abandoning it, than to undermine it from within, hollowing it out, draining it of its ideological force and its moral energy. In other words, parody was already an important element of his dramatic strategy; so was provocation. For, while Pinter's work may have perplexed and disturbed the West End audience, Orton's provoked it.

His first stage play, *Entertaining Mr Sloane*, was denounced by the more reactionary elements in the commercial theatre, and in particular by one of the directors of a booking agency. It was attacked in the press, a process Orton obligingly helped along in a letter to the *Daily Telegraph* which appeared under his favourite pseudonym, 'Edna Welthorpe (Mrs)'. Even Sean O'Casey disliked its subject and tone, though his description of it as 'A play to make a man pull his trousers up'[10] would have appealed to Orton. Its amoral character, its indelicate collage of homosexuality, nymphomania and incest, and its casual violence, provoked a response rivalled only by Edward Bond's *Saved*, in which a baby in a pram is stoned to death. Indeed, in a book about a famous murder case of the sixties, the 'Moors murders' (*On Iniquity*, 1967), Pamela Hansford Johnson indicted both plays for compounding a rising tide of violence, for elevating the psychopath to the position of exemplar – a realistic reading which may have some relevance to Bond's play but which is simply an attempt to recuperate a realism that Orton had carefully evacuated from his text. For him, as for Robbe-Grillet, 'The serious attitude presupposes that there is something behind our gestures: a soul, a god, values, the bourgeois order . . . whereas behind the game there is nothing . . . the game offers itself as purely gratuitous.'[11] Described by Christopher Butler as a commonplace of French postmodernism, this had not been a feature of English writing – except perhaps in that tradition of comic writing to which Orton tended to relate himself.

Pinter's subversions were of a rather different kind. He baffled audiences; he did not taunt them. He did not challenge central taboos. His language, for the most part, was not scatological, his characters not so sexually anarchic. Indeed, when he did stray into this area, in *The Homecoming*, Orton claimed that it was as a result of his influence (though Pinter denies this). Nor was the parodic element as strong.

Of course, parody is an ambiguous weapon. Ostensibly it offers the audience a reassuring sense of superiority, a knowing complicity with the author. It flatters them with the assumption that they share a command of the models being subverted and are fully aware of the nature of those subversions. But Orton played a double game. Though his apparent models were the detective story, the melodrama and the light comedy, his other paradigms were buried deeper: classical drama, Restoration wit, Wildean paradox. Indeed, he relied on his audience's failing to recognize the parodic thrust and took pleasure in their discomfiture. The superiority of the writer over his characters mirrored a superiority of writer over audience in which he delighted. Relying on the ignorance of those he goaded, he needed the bourgeois audience to allow him the *frisson* that derives from delivering public insults with impunity. The baffled rage of audiences and critics merely heightened his own self-regard and sanctioned his own actions, which became not simply hedonistic exploits but gestures of freedom. The narcissist is only apparently self-sufficient; he needs an audience to confirm his own self-regard. And Orton certainly was such a narcissist.

*

His first plays, then, picture an antinomian world inhabited by spiritually debilitated characters, a world that is not so much a product of social forces as productive of them. In his subsequent work, however, he tended to become what Albee once described himself as being, a demonic social critic, as he focuses on the temporal agents of that determinism, the authoritarian figures who conspire to project metaphysical absurdity on to a social level. In his final plays he celebrates the splendidly anarchistic spirit that is liberated by absurdity, rather than delineating the ever-diminishing world of human action as Beckett had done. The sober madness of his earlier work gives way to the manic energy of the later. Sexuality is no longer seen as the painful source of human frustration and violence but as an absurdly trivial activity, the fit subject for a reductive humour. ('There is no finer sight', the female personnel officer in *The Good and Faithful Servant* observes, 'than two married people making love', p. 182.) Orton, in other words, presses the absurd towards farce – a movement that gathered pace after the most socially conscious of his absurdist plays, *The Good and Faithful Servant*.

While there is clearly a social dimension to plays that describe the world of diminished human possibilities, the deterioration of human relationships and the fragility of language, this is not his main concern in the early plays. For here he sees the metaphysical world as projecting a more fundamental dissonance than that which defines the individual's relationship to the social world. In a sense, of course, one could say much the same of Ibsen, who recognized clearly enough that gulf between aspiration and performance which is the basis both of the naturalist impulse and the absurdist perception. The social world in Ibsen is simply the form in which that determinism is expressed – not the source of that determinism. The pain felt by his heroes and heroines has little to do with women's rights, the need for integrity in public life, or the danger of concealing painful incidents from the past; it comes, rather, directly out of the wound which, as Beckett well knew, opened up at the moment of birth – the moment, after all, that separates the individual from the Platonic idea, the first of the many ironies that form the shifting realities with which his protagonists must deal.

This is no less true of Orton, whose subject is equally man's alienation from himself. What has changed is that Ibsen's conviction of an attainable identity, of the possibility of autonomous action, has disappeared. As far as Orton was concerned, Ibsen's liberal world has gone. Ibsen's Nora strides out of the door, no longer to be contained either by bourgeois society or by the art with which it protects itself from the real. Yet, like the child who leaves home at an angry word from its parent, such heroes are fated to return; for not only does history force them back into time, which is itself a shaper of moral worlds, but their own ethical awareness drives them to accept responsibility for the Other as for the Self. This social responsibility begins in guilt and crystallizes in social action – hence the presumption that Ibsen is a writer of 'social plays'. If Nora's door were to remain for ever closed, this new sense of self must necessarily collapse, having nothing against which it can define itself. A world of Bartlebys building their lives on refusal, living out an absurdist reality, would leave no world beyond the confines of the individual imagination. For Ibsen, man is decidedly a social animal: though the essence of the world with which he deals is metaphysical, he cannot envisage man separated from a social context.

For Orton, however, Nora's act is without meaning, since the world on the other side of the door differs in no important respects from that on this side. There is no residual identity to which the individual may retreat, and society is nothing more than the name given to the brutal interplay of competing desires. His characters are not simply alienated from post-industrial society; they are alienated from themselves. Ibsen believes that the primal wound can be healed; Orton sees no prospect of this. Even *in extremis* Ibsen's characters can explain themselves to themselves; Orton's characters can only deploy the empty phrases they have picked up from the public definers of reality ('I'm sorry you've been troubled', 'Make your enquiries elsewhere', 'You've no evidence to support your theory', 'She tells of her night of terror').

The 'meaning' of Orton's plays is clearly not recuperable primarily from an account of their plots or even a description of their characters. To a far greater extent than usual, the style of these plays, their wit and their internal processes are their meaning. Causalities are suppressed or mocked, the significance of action is dissipated, coherences dissolve, the presumed logic of moral process is disrupted and warped. *The Good and Faithful Servant*, therefore, is something of an exception in his work. It is a satire; and this implies something of a moral stance on Orton's part. The characters are what society has made them: they are infantilized, mechanized, quite literally demoralized by a system that values only its own processes. The protagonist, Buchanan, works for a company so large that he goes unrecognized and has a hard time finding his way through the labyrinth of its corridors. But the sense of anger here which generates Orton's satire is unique in a career more usually given to mocking the assumption that presentation conceals representation.

Once again the protagonist is a marginal man – is, that is to say, the prototypical hero of contemporary drama. Buchanan is about to retire from the company for which he has worked for fifty years, half a century of loyal service having won him the job of commissionaire, in which position he once opened the door for the Chairman of the Board (a boast clearly akin to that of one of Rabbit's friends and relations, in A. A. Milne's *The House at Pooh Corner*, that he might once have seen Christopher Robin's foot only wasn't exactly sure). The whole paraphernalia of social welfare and public relations (today's substitute for personal relations: human contact professionalized and conducted for financial reward), welded together in the person of Mrs Vealfoy, swings effortlessly into action, concealing fundamental indifference behind the trappings of minor ceremony. But as he is about to leave, in a parody of Hollywood's sentimental chance encounters, he meets Edith, an old cleaning woman, whom he discovers to be the girl he had once made pregnant – itself an unhappy consequence of the fact that the path to her house lay through a field of inconveniently convenient tall grass. There follows a wry account of the subsequent career of the twin offspring – particularly of what Ed, in *Entertaining Mr Sloane*, would have called their vaginalatrous experiences. We learn that the child resulting from the extramarital relations between one or other or both of these boys and a foreign woman of equally uncertain morals is now living with Edith, whose own fifty years of loyal service have left her with the bucket and cloth with which she had started. The revelation of the existence of this grandchild, who is himself, incidentally, continuing the family tradition of promiscuous fornication, throws a temporary spanner into the company's welfare machinery. But since it ultimately thrives on precisely such human disasters, which provide the justification for its existence, it recovers with admirable speed, rendering harmless even such slender evidence of autonomous action by locating the appropriate form, uttering the requisite clichés, legitimizing the aberrant act. In this world there can be no room for individual initiative, which serves only to mess up the paperwork and disrupt the schedules.

In Mrs Vealfoy's world everything is classifiable, all pain can apparently be relieved, all wounds ostensibly be healed: for the injured there is the company doctor, for the lonely the social club, for the pregnant a company wedding, for the dead a company tribute. There is no space left for individuality, no misguided independence that cannot be immediately absorbed. Orton's ironic view is directed not only at corporate capitalism but at the great unsocial present we each separately inhabit. Manipulated from birth, forced to adapt our sense of selfhood to the ready-made identities of the public world, we render absurdity doubly absurd, allowing habit and custom, utility and expediency, to become the only principles we can acknowledge, and nerveless passivity before an externally defined life to be the only philosophy to which we are prepared to grant any dignity. No alternative is offered by Mrs Vealfoy, because this is a society that has conspired to destroy such alternatives, and the awareness of alternatives. But there is a residual perception, one that can be expressed not in language – language has itself long since been captured by the authorities and rendered harmless – but in momentary acts of blind rage and bewilderment. Buchanan, lost, lonely, betrayed by his own values, hits out in the only way he can: he smashes the clock and the toaster the company had presented to him on his retirement, for these are the inadequate but tangible symbols of the inconsequence of his life and of the completeness with which time and existence have been defined by forces other than his own emotional integrity. It is an anarchic gesture of the kind Orton respected, for he, with Kenneth Halliwell, wanted 'to smash the wretched civilization'.[12]

In the words of the *Concise Oxford Dictionary*, which Orton prints as an epigraph to the play, the only faith Buchanan had been allowed has been defined in terms of his 'trust in authority'. It is that which has betrayed him, which has infantilized him and his fellow members of the Bright Hours Club. There is no transcendence in his life, certainly none in his death. He dies in the middle of someone else's conversation, no more positive in his leaving of life than in his living of it. The world is essentially that described by Jung in his study of the systematic destruction of the individual, *The Undiscovered Self*, a book that explores an increasingly authoritarian state machinery which in the name of social welfare erodes individual autonomy:

The individual, and, indeed, all individual events whatsoever, suffer a levelling down and a process of blurring that distorts the picture of reality into a conceptual average. . . . Instead of moral and mental differentiation of the individual, you have public welfare and the raising of the living standard. The goal and meaning of individual life (which is the only *real* life) no longer lie in individual development. . . . The individual is increasingly deprived of the moral decision as to how he should live his own life. . . . The rulers, in their turn, are just as much social units. . . . They do not need to be personalities capable of judgement . . .[13]

It was just this world that Orton rebelled against, not by seeking to reconstruct a moral world, but, in his private and artistic life, by praising the aberrant, subverting the real and deploying a series of personae immune to assault because of their pure fictionality.

Perhaps, as Christopher Lasch has argued of America, a reaction against the authoritarian family, a repressive censorship and the work ethic misses the point, since these are already in an advanced state of decay. Certainly, short though it was, Orton's life was long enough for him to witness the collapse of part at least of this edifice. And, as Marcuse was to observe, society showed a remarkable ability to draw from sexual licence and anarchic lifestyles the energy it had once drawn from repression and conformity. Contrariwise, Orton, who attacked industrial exploitation and a reductive capitalism in *The Good and Faithful Servant*, was quite prepared to apply its ethics himself in the sexual-commodity market: commodity values are not so much overthrown as simply reconstituted in sensual terms. Indeed, while writing his diatribe against the reduction of the body to mere instrument by capitalist society, his diary entries were celebrating the instrumentality of sex, the accumulated property of his sexual conquests, not only listing in detail the physical properties of his one-night stands but taking pride in the number as well as the nature of these relationships. It was, however, a contradiction in which he exulted.

3

ANARCHIC FARCE

Loot, completed in October 1964, was the first evidence of a shift in Orton's work away from the Pinter-influenced absurdism of the early plays to the absurdist world of anarchic farce. It was very clearly an act of public revenge for the humiliations society had inflicted upon him in an equally public way. He said in a letter to the actor-comedian Kenneth Williams, 'I'm writing a play to show all the inanities and stupidities I've undergone.'[14] It was a play that very deliberately set out to flout all normal standards of good taste, an objective that did little to assure its stage success. It ridiculed the hypocrisy of polite society and exposed the cant of authority. The characters, with a single exception, are all totally corrupt, creating among themselves the only kind of society Orton seemed to believe possible: a society of the self-seeking.

But once again his most studied blows were reserved for the figures of authority, more especially for the police who, as a drug-taking homosexual, he regarded as a natural enemy, a necessary evil perhaps, but an image of all the restrictions into which he had run full-tilt over the years. For he was supremely conscious of living in a country in which, as one of the characters in *Loot* explains, 'respect for the law is proverbial', where, in fact, people would willingly 'give power of arrest to the traffic lights if three women magistrates and a Liberal MP would only suggest it' (p. 248). The plot is, indeed, a neat reversal of the standard mystery play, a parody of that restoration of order which is inherent in the detective story and the well-made realistic play alike.

Hal, a dissolute young man of uncertain sexual leanings,

41

having robbed a bank with an assistant undertaker of like character (Dennis), secretes the proceeds in his mother's coffin, which is conveniently to hand. In order to accomplish this, however, he is forced to remove the corpse and in doing so is detected by his mother's nurse, Fay. Since she is anyway of a lascivious and larcenous nature, with inclinations that run in the direction of blackmail and murder rather than geriatrics, he enlists her help. She readily agrees, since she regards this as a convenient bonus on top of the money she hopes she will derive from marrying Mr McLeavy, husband of the woman she has just poisoned and already marked down as the next in an ever-lengthening list of victims.

It rapidly proves more difficult for this gang of criminals to escape with the loot than they had imagined, partly because Hal suffers from a pathological need to tell the truth, partly because Inspector Truscott of Scotland Yard appears on the scene to take advantage of this unfortunate character defect. Truscott goes about the task with which society has entrusted him with enthusiasm, if with a somewhat low regard for the niceties of police procedure. In order to circumvent what he sees as inconvenient restrictions on his freedom of action, he masquerades as an inspector of the Metropolitan Water Board, a body not charged by law with justifying its arbitrary actions in the same way as the police. Betrayed by an errant glass eye, which inconveniently pops out of the maternal corpse, thereby making it increasingly difficult for them to sustain their suggestion that the bandaged body is in fact no more than a dressmaker's dummy, they are forced to offer the police inspector a bribe. This he accepts, and, in order to avoid any awkward questions from the increasingly suspicious McLeavy, he arrests him on a trumped-up charge. Thus injustice wins the day, leaving the inspector free to take his wife on a trip to see the tulip fields of Holland, Hal free to invest his money in a brothel, and Dennis free to marry the homicidal nurse.

The only character with any sense of moral values, with any scruples that are not up for sale to the highest bidder, is McLeavy, and he is systematically insulted and abused. His touching faith in authority ('As a good citizen I ignore the stories which bring officialdom into disrepute', p. 217) simply makes him a more convenient victim for the rapacious grotesques around him. When he insists that 'the police are for the protection of ordinary people', the police inspector can only reply in disbelief, 'I don't know where you pick up these slogans, sir. You must read them on the hoardings' (p. 274).

This is no longer an existence operating according to logical principles, and consequently reason can offer no defence against the arbitrary. Truscott is clearly simply living out the contingent nature of his world in spelling out his Catch 22 logic to McLeavy:

TRUSCOTT. I'm an official of the Metropolitan Water Board
. . .
MCLEAVY. But the water board has no power to keep law-abiding citizens confined to their rooms.
TRUSCOTT. Not if the citizens are law abiding.
MCLEAVY. Whether they're law abiding or not the water board has no power.
TRUSCOTT. I don't propose to argue hypothetical cases with you, sir. Remain where you are till further notice.
MCLEAVY. I shall take legal advice.
TRUSCOTT. That is as may be. I've no power to prevent you.
MCLEAVY. I want to telephone my lawyer.
TRUSCOTT. I can't allow you to do that. It would be contrary to regulations. We've no case against you. (p. 240)

When McLeavy asks, with an edge of desperation, 'Is the world mad? Tell me it's not', Truscott can only reply, 'I'm not paid to quarrel with accepted facts' (p. 258). And here, in fact, is a clue to the world that Orton creates. For he does indeed describe a world that has descended into unreality, so that Fay's concluding comment, 'We must keep up appearances' (p. 275), is not to be taken simply as a parody of middle-class hypocrisy. It is in fact a prescription for survival. In a world lacking in moral substance, the image may indeed be the only reality, a fictionalizing self the only protection against being trapped in the monolithic fiction of the state.

In this respect Orton's later plays are more thoroughgoingly subversive than the earlier ones, for farce becomes not merely a form of realism but a strategy to ensure survival. As he indicated in *Entertaining Mr Sloane* and *The Ruffian on the Stair*, the great risk is to be committed, to accept seriousness as a possible response to one's surroundings. His last works not merely present the fluid, confusing, amoral, neurotic, posturing world of contemporary existence; they celebrate it. It is in this sense that he regarded *Loot* as 'a plea against compartmentalization'.[15] His characters are a series of 'performed selves' who evade the painful realities of existence by refusing to treat them with any seriousness, refusing to grant any connection between the roles they play and any other self which may be capable of suffering the ultimate traumas of birth and death. For Erving Goffman, the 'performed self' was not

> an organic thing that has a specific location, whose fundamental fate is to be born, to mature, and to die, it is a dramatic effect arising diffusely from a scene that is presented, and the characteristic issue, the crucial concern, is whether it will be credited or discredited.[16]

Thus, too, in farce attention shifts from change deriving from the egregious circumstances of life and death to change deriving purely from the shifting perspectives and circumstances of social misunderstandings.

In his own life his belief that there is no irreducible self, that there is no end to the process of unmaking which is the stuff of human existence, led him to substitute quantity for quality (piling up sensual experience with the avidity of Camus's Caligula), selves for self, discovering in the shifting identities of his protagonists both an appropriate image of contemporary role playing and, ultimately, a possible strategy for escaping those who wished to pigeon-hole him as homosexual, bohemian, drug taker, hedonist. The more roles he amassed, the harder it was to tie him down to any of them. He himself adopted various personae ('Donald H. Hartley' and 'Edna Welthorpe', among others) in letters to institutions and public figures, while even his first name was changed from John to Joe (primarily to avoid any possible confusion with John Osborne). He was a habitual user of drugs, and it is possible, I think, to see this too as a retreat from public identity, as the expression of a desire to dismantle a clearly defined self; for, as the American writer Jerzy Kosinski has suggested, drugs 'smash the mirror of personal identity'.[17] But in his work such strategies merely underline absurdity. In *Loot* death is a sick

44

joke having no human content at all. The body is an object with no more human connection than the dressmaker's dummy it is purported to be. Stripped of its teeth and glass eye, it is 'filleted without a qualm' by its adoring husband. It becomes an object like any other, a prop – an image of the body as object which is an essential presumption of farce as a form. This fascination, indeed, was as evident in life as in art. Orton's sister, Leonie, has said:

> He nearly had mother out of her coffin. . . . He was picking her head up. 'What's all this brown stuff?'; 'try and get her rings off'. I said 'I don't want to.' He said, 'I do.' He wanted to see her feet, he was opening her dressing gown. 'It's incredible,' he said, 'doesn't she look bizarre.' The kids were screaming and I said, 'For Christ's sake leave her alone.'[18]

*

The Erpingham Camp, written for television in 1965 (for transmission in 1966) and produced on the stage, in revised form, by the Royal Court in June 1967, was very much in the new style that had emerged with *Loot*. Beneath the humour, which now deliberately smashes all pretence at realism, there is a mordant observer dispassionately remarking on the absurdity of all human passion and action. Mankind is seen as a scrabbling mass of grotesque creatures, uncomprehendingly enacting public roles in which they have been hopelessly miscast. *The Erpingham Camp* presents a Hieronymus Bosch world in which pain and degradation are the common currency, and the only structure is that imposed by the consistency of suffering or by the arbitrary act of the artist in choosing to locate the frenzied activity within a recognizable dramatic frame. It is a comedy of dislocation, an anarchic farce in which the sustaining myths of human rationality, dignity and integrity are seen as illusory. The view of human nature exposed here is much the same as that captured by the late Goya sketches: man as uncomprehending brute. Thus, despite the eponymous hero's proud assertion that 'we live in a rational world' (p. 282), the evidence of the play consistently contradicts him. For it consists of an elaborate act of decreation on the part of its characters as they enact the entropic process common to Orton's plays, as it is to the human organism itself. Faced with this ineluctable process, Erpingham can only exert an authority which is a substitute for will or fall back on what he calls the 'best in twentieth century civilization'. But, since this turns out to be 'Russ Conway on the gram and a browse through a James Bond' (p. 308), it proves a somewhat fragile resource.

The play is set in a holiday camp ruled with inflexible authority and quixotic inconsistency by Erpingham, who has the grace to be as contemptuous of his staff as he is of his campers. He is a man of vision, though the nature of that vision is prosaically commercial, as he envisages Entertainment Centres strategically located on National Trust property with drum majorettes marching regularly across the rapidly diminishing unspoiled countryside of Britain. To assist him in entertaining the campers, who seem at first indistinguishable from one another in their stupidity, he has a staff of moral and physical incompetents, the padre having just returned from a court appearance in which he had been charged with assaulting a young girl, and the Chief Redcoat being dangerously inadequate, precipitating the riot that destroys the camp. As a satire on church and state, conveniently allied as they are here in their spiritual and secular objectives, it is telling, if a touch unsubtle. Figures of authority are indelicately deflated. A nun who becomes Sister Superior is described as falling to the ground in the middle of the Te Deum mouthing words only understood by a young lay sister who in her more worldly days had been an usherette at the Roxy Cinema. Erpingham himself is made to plunge to his death through a hole in the floor, thereby killing a young couple who have the ill-luck to be dancing in the hall below.

The ceremonies with which authority validates its existence, the rituals employed to justify the continued dominance of the power élite, are mocked throughout. When Chief Redcoat Riley receives the ultimate accolade, being made Entertainments Organizer, the installation becomes a mock coronation, accompanied by a traditional rendition of 'Zadok the Priest' and a less traditional 'unearthly radiance' which serves to draw God too into Orton's subversive world. This epiphany is concluded by a jingoistic invocation of the glorious history of the British Empire, undermined only by Riley's inconvenient insistence that he had been born in Ireland. Thus is government assisted by a bungling bureaucracy whose job is to ensure the passive acquiescence of the populace by the provision of the appropriate bread and circuses. In this task Riley is assisted by Jessie Mason and W. E. Harrison, who double as entertainers and food tasters, and preside over the collapse of their world with the fixed grins and servile loyalty of functionaries the world around.

Yet, if Orton's contempt for authority is clear enough in a play that manages incidentally to ridicule the Queen, military pomp, nationalist fervour and the cant of politicians, he has no more confidence in the rebel. Indeed, *The Erpingham Camp* offers a mordant satire on the heroics of Establishment and revolutionary alike. It stands as a rejection of the whole world of politics and social action. The revolutionaries themselves are urged to action not by some radical affront to social justice but by the mistaken belief that Riley's over-vigorous cure for the hysterical state of one of the guests is in fact a violent assault. Defending some ponderous notion of gentility and an even less distinctly perceived sense of social propriety, they instantly resort to stereotypical roles.

At the heart of the revolt lie a middle-class pair, Lou and Ted, stalwarts of the civil defence, proud owners of an inherited semi-detached and a sun lamp, and one of whom had been honoured to be invited to keep the score in a table tennis match in which the daughter of a brain specialist was to perform; the others, Kenny and Eileen, are a working-class couple whose instinctive violence is presented as a substitute for the language which for the most part they are so signally incapable of deploying. Eileen's contribution to the evening's social inter-course is the announcement that 'My mum was on a lecture once. She could tell you a thing or two. They exhibited her as a reference. . . . And although they got our love forbidden and made life not worth living, I'm pregnant now and they've been good parents' (p. 286). Having delivered herself of this series of non sequiturs and grammatical impossibilities, she collapses in tears. Ted, on the other hand, is a middle-class reformist and accordingly wishes to proceed with caution, to employ nego-tiation, to resort to the law. He and his wife try to take control of the situation on the somewhat dubious grounds that they are civil defence workers. But Kenny urges on his motley troop of campers with a cry that is a parody of the slogans that have, over the centuries, sent millions of people to their death: 'Have a bash, I say. Have a bash for the pregnant woman next door' (p. 310). Ted and Lou's rationality is greeted with an invitation to 'Piss off you dirty middle-class prat . . . before I kick your dental plate to pieces' (p. 311), a class insult so finely calculated that the then functioning Lord Chamberlain saw fit to demand its removal from the script, presumably on the grounds that its inclusion would indeed prove disturbing to those middle-class people who conventionally form most theatre audiences.

And so the revolution is launched with a familiar enough speech from its radical leader:

> I'm an ordinary man – I've no wish to be a leader – my only ambition is to rest in peace by my own fireside. But in the life of every one of us, there comes a time when he must choose – whether to be treated in the manner of the bad old days. Or whether to take by force those common human rights which should be denied to no man. (p. 309)

This fluent defence of human rights is undermined only by the fact that it is delivered by a man wearing a leopard skin (having been persuaded to do so as part of the evening's festivities), whose idea of common human rights consists of gaining access to his holiday camp chalet and to the cold meat and trifle which Erpingham has thoughtfully withheld as a sanction against the recalcitrant campers. The inappropriateness of the rhetoric suggests that this kind of off-the-peg diatribe exists wholly independently of the cause to which it seems attached. Its very appeal to abstract values is offered as an indication of its universal utility and thus of its inherent dishonesty, the more so since it turns out simply to be a rationalization for vindictive violence.

Erpingham's response to the forces of revolution, who have already set fire to the Grand Ballroom and assumed the various privileges of revolution (namely rape and plunder), is to threaten the rebels with retribution, reminding them that in his view they 'have no rights', only 'certain privileges which can be withdrawn'. Assuming the awful power of authority, he then announces: 'I am withdrawing them.' It is a familiar stage in revolutionary skirmishing, as authority seeks to assert its waning power. And the response is equally familiar as Kenny announces, 'You'll pay for this, you ignorant fucker!' (p. 307), a reply specifically designed as an act of *lèse-majesté*, and one that the ever-sensitive Lord Chamberlain clearly perceived as such, for this, too, was excised from the text. By degrees his staff desert, the loss of medical officer, chief engineer, security officer and the woman on the postcard stand being seen by Erpingham as the collapse of medicine, science, defence and the liberal arts. He finally falls back on the invocation of principles no less ambiguous than those addressed by his enemies. 'If we stand firm by the principles on which this camp was founded,' he suggests, 'the clouds will pass', since the whole episode has only 'been fermented by a handful of intellectuals' (p. 308). The inappropriateness of these remarks is painfully clear. The rebels would after all scarcely understand the meaning of the word intellectual, while the principles behind the founding of the camp have been nothing more noble than greed and the pathological pursuit of power.

The play draws to a close in a welter of violence which seems, if nothing else, to cast considerable doubt on Erpingham's earlier-expressed opinion that the parable of the swine has no 'real meaning for us today'. Clearly, what Orton has offered us has been precisely a new parable of the swine, though this time the devils have not been granted the dispensation of a retreat into the pigs; rather, their human hosts have themselves become manic animals rushing to destruction.

The move from *The Ruffian on the Stair* and *Entertaining Mr Sloane* to *Loot*, *The Erpingham Camp* and *What the Butler Saw* was a retreat from mystery, from implied depth, from density. In escaping Pinter's influence, Orton opted for a world in which his primary weapons became parody, sexual affront, visual and verbal humour and macabre juxtaposition. He learned from Pinter the need to treat the bizarre as simple realism and recognized the humour to be derived from a disproportion between social class and linguistic register; but, where Pinter aimed at a questioning of ontological status, Orton was concerned with a dislocation of the sensibility and turned his work into an act of aggression which did not stop at the boundaries of art.

*

In many respects Orton was more profoundly revolutionary than those playwrights who immediately preceded him, and who had been presented as bringing about radical changes in English theatre. Unlike them, he was as suspicious of dramatic form as he was of social imperatives. He set out to undermine both. Not so the Osbornes and Weskers who had defined the nature of theatrical revolt in the late fifties and early sixties. Wesker's and Osborne's iconoclasm was, to a degree, illusory – a renewal of naturalism, albeit responding to a profound sense of social and moral dislocation. Orton was prepared to taunt his audience with the disturbing thought that only disorder can generate vitality and a compelling humour – that true liberation may lie in cutting loose from the moral world rather than trying to reconstruct it, in abandoning liberal notions of individual identity and social responsibility. Authority of any kind becomes a vicious and dehumanizing force. It serves only to frustrate an individual performance which is as much a reality as the fictions of society itself. The role playing to be found in the theatre is no longer contrasted with 'real life' but offered as an immediate strategy for those assailed by demands for social conformity. The authority of the camp owner, in *The Erpingham Camp*, is best opposed not by rational complaint and the assertion of legal rights but by a riot which, significantly, starts on a stage (the origin of Orton's own riotous subversion); the petulant demands of the Ministry-appointed psychiatrist, in *What the Butler Saw*, are frustrated not by a rigid adherence to norms of behaviour but by a disturbingly flexible approach to identity, with the characters repeatedly changing their roles as easily as they change their clothes.

Yet this is not simply a defence against the intrusive demands of society: it is, at base, a comment upon that society. For the artificial world of Orton's plays – a world in which character is provisional, violence imminent, language unreliable, reality uncertain – constitutes both a metaphysical observation and an image of contemporary life as he saw it. But, where society deliberately constructs a series of values which it then regards as absolute, Orton's protagonists behave as though the world were the antinomian place that Orton himself takes it to be. If they recognize the existence of social standards and sometimes pay them an ironic regard, their own energy is sustained not by observing the rules of the social contract but by playing their changing roles with vigour and commitment. Orton's plays have the virtue of confessing to their artificiality, their fictiveness.

The mood of English drama, and in fact the English novel, may seem to have changed in the fifties and early sixties, but there was still an emphasis on reconciliation, order and restoration. The bitterness of the working class and the anger of the new professional class now found expression, but the tone was one of bewilderment rather than revolt. Osborne could identify with devastating accuracy the 'nothing very much thank you' society of the fifties, but he offered nothing with which to replace it. Indeed, in both *Look Back in Anger* and *The Entertainer* it is the representatives of the old order who seem to compel a grudging but real admiration; they at least are the products of a world in which people could behave as though there were fixed points, even if this were an illusion. If such a conviction did not in fact seem credible to Osborne, he could identify no resource beyond a studied romanticism with which to neutralize the enervated spirit of his bitterly asocial world: as for so many other protagonists in the novels and plays of the fifties, there is nothing left for Osborne's characters except a pained and knowing acceptance of the diminished world of modern realism.

Wesker's newly committed class heroes, awakening to a sense of social urgency which seemed otherwise to have died with the fall of Spain, searching for an adequate response to continued privilege and a prosaic capitalism, were quickly stifled by the bland atmosphere of welfare-state anonymity. Their romantic assumptions for the most part broke pointlessly against the banality of contemporary life. The new playwrights captured the texture of society with greater honesty than before, but no serious doubts were cast on the need for authority, for social institutions, for a system against which the individual could prove himself and define an identity. They were searching in one way or another for some form of certainty, some structure that would make sense of the neurotic compulsions of modern life; their art was both an expression of this need and itself a paradigm of the structured world they sought. But neither art nor society could bear the weight. The liberal presumptions of Osborne and Wesker seemed to many outdated and untrue. By contrast, playwrights like Beckett (if an Irishman writing in French can be claimed for English drama) and Pinter detected a metaphysical insecurity beneath the social concerns of their contemporaries. The universal descent into unreality that has typified post-modernist literature surfaces in contemporary English drama as a fragmented world in which characters, purged of the rounded reality of liberal drama, move uncertainly or even obliviously through a strange landscape whose strangeness must simply be accepted. This is the world of Beckett's and Pinter's plays, as it is of Stoppard's *Rosencrantz and Guildenstern Are Dead*. It is also the world created by Joe Orton, who actually lived out the absurdity of his age, an age he could never take entirely seriously but which always threatened to devolve into violence and death – as, eventually, it did in reality for him.

The inhumanity of modern life is no longer countered by the assertion of liberal values but rather by a neutralizing madness or marginality. And the form embraced has frequently been that which defines itself by reference to marginality and inconsequence: farce, a new form of anarchic force derived from a wedding of the absurd and the old farce tradition. The original meaning of the word, indeed, implies inessential material, padding used to conceal a void or a silence. Hence the word applied both to the stuffing of a game bird and the various liturgical formulas that punctuated a priest's prayers. The protagonists of this new farce-world are therefore themselves marginal, irrelevant to the slow unwinding of an entropic process, while the form itself is self-destructive, implying the existence of no Platonic idea in the mad logic of its own configurations. Indeed, entropy – a term drawn from thermodynamics and signifying the degree of disorder in a system, the progressive loss of energy in a machine – is as useful in an account of Orton's work as it is in a consideration of that of the American novelist Thomas Pynchon. For disorder characterizes both their worlds, as a progressive dismantling marks their characters (in Orton's case they are stripped or injured and even die). For both writers order is a phantom, the source of an irony that defines human experience.

If Orton was in some ways a representative of the post-modernist impulse, then it is worth recalling that post-modernism has two faces. On the one hand, it identifies the collapse of form, the loss of meaning, contingency, stasis, a marginality that is equally the product of social alienation and metaphysical abandonment; on the other, it celebrates that marginality, sees experience as a dimension of aesthetics, rejoices in the ludic and generates a manic energy. Orton, who began his career, under the influence of Pinter and Beckett (the two contemporary writers whom he most respected), as an exemplar of the former mode, ended as an embodiment of the latter. And in that he was very much an expression of his times. His stress on the sensual rather than the intellectual (though his wit plainly relied on intellectual processes), on an insurgency that derived from his own marginal position, his membership of a menaced subculture, was not merely widely shared but became itself something of an orthodoxy, more especially in America. In a book published in 1967 Susan Sontag insisted that art is essentially an expression of energy and sensual capability. Herbert Marcuse and Norman O. Brown identified art with the victory of the pleasure principle over the reality principle: a polymorphous sexuality was to be the key to rebellion. The body was pitched against the machine. And so, for a while, it was in the mid-sixties, when the avant-garde theatre was under the influence of Antonin Artaud (deeply suspicious of a rational, moralizing theatre), Britain (at the behest of *Time* magazine) celebrated its 'swinging' image, and the nude body, in street and theatre, was presented as a symbol of authenticity and rebellion. Play became a central strategy, a refusal of seriousness being seen as a primary means of release.

Orton's work, and in particular the later plays, seems to reflect such convictions, to rest on the assumption that life is an elaborate performance, a fiction in which characters contain no more depth or reality than is demanded by the conventions of their role or permitted by the exigencies of social organiza-tion. In one sense this is to say no more than that Orton is indeed a *farceur*, for the world of farce is of course a world of partial beings, role players whose mask is constantly in danger of slipping, even if this is conveniently reinstated at the climax of the play. But here Orton differs. His social charades are made of sterner stuff. His characters cannot be so conveniently

53

restored to their featureless norm as can the heroes of old farce; their wounds cannot be cauterized by a graceful arabesque of plot. They struggle to sustain illusions of purposeful existence with nothing more elaborate than a tissue of language.

If in farce action is substituted for feeling until human relations are little more than the extruded consequence of circumstance, in Orton's work the assault launched on individual character by the representatives of authority and normality is not without an edge of viciousness and a residual pathos. If this is farce, it is Pinter played as farce.

*

The only logic Orton could detect was the mad, circular logic of dementia; the only art he wished to generate, one that undermined models of social and artistic order. In the wildly absurd *Funeral Games*, presented by Yorkshire Television in 1968, he created a bewilderingly complex plot which turns on a neat reversal of conventional morality, the baroque arabesques of plot detail constituting an ironic comment on the narrative tradition in literature and, more significantly, presumptions of human rationality and spiritual integrity.

Pringle, a self-styled Bishop of the Brotherhood, a hedonistic community seemingly created to rationalize his own sexual voracity, employs a private inquiry agent and nude model, Caulfield, to investigate his wife's supposed infidelity. She is a health visitor and is providing private treatment of a somewhat ambiguous kind to McCorquodale, an impotent man whose bodily functions have all but ceased. A one-time Catholic priest and convert to the Brotherhood, McCorquodale had been excommunicated by Pringle when the former had discovered him in the process of celebrating various supposedly spiritual but actually pornographic rites with his wife. With admirable ecumenicism, McCorquodale is now a member of a salvationist assembly and, fearful that his own wife, Val, may one day end up 'leering round my death bed', has taken the precaution of a pre-emptive murder. She now rests in his cellar 'under a ton of smokeless' fuel.

Pringle, since his religious reputation depends on his willingness to extort swift retribution from his supposedly adulterous wife ('Thou shalt not suffer an adulteress to live'), persuades her to acquiesce in a rumour that he has in fact killed her. This results in his acquiring a reputation as a just and fearless Christian. Unfortunately a sceptical investigative journalist doubts his rigour, and he is obliged to furnish evidence of the crime he has not committed. Caulfield obliges by hacking a hand off the dead body of McCorquodale's wife. When Pringle's wife discovers the murder, the victim being a long-term friend of hers, she is herself tied up preparatory to her own demise. At this point Pringle arrives and he and his one-time acolyte struggle, McCorquodale threatening to make public his ex-superior's lack of homicidal conviction. When the police fortuitously arrive, Pringle volunteers the wholly erroneous information that the body in the basement is in fact that of his wife, thus restoring his public reputation.

It is scarcely any wonder that one of the play's characters should confess that he has 'learned to accept the irrational in everyday life' (p. 332). For this is a world in which 'the humble and meek are thirsting for blood' (p. 337), in which the church, whose ironic symbol is a bird of prey carrying an olive branch, is seen as merely a cover for violence. It is a world stood on its head, a place of mad logic, a frenzied correlative of a contemporary existence whose own style can perhaps best be described as neurotic. Like the complex interleaving conspiracies of Thomas Pynchon, which parody the compulsive human search for meaning and structure, it offers evidence of nothing but its own internal form. It is an impossible world, but one that is painfully close to our own in which religion has all too often proved simply another face of self-interest and violence, in which the existence of structured actions has been taken as evidence of cosmic meaning. Here the patterns are clearly self-destructive, wholly unrelated to any concept of reality or truth. Indeed, when one of the characters announces that 'Truth must win. Otherwise life is impossible' (p. 355), this is simply a prelude to the blatant lie with which the play ends. The conclusion is clear. Life is indeed impossible, and if Pringle's final remark is accurate – 'Everything works out in accordance with the divine Will' (p. 360) – then it is clear that this gulf between aspiration and reality is endemic.

*

It is entirely appropriate that Orton's last play, *What the Butler Saw*, should be set in a mental hospital, for a consistent theme of his work is essentially that implied in the words from *The Revenger's Tragedy* which form its epigraph: 'Surely we're all mad people, and they whom we think are, are not.' Like the *Marat/Sade* or *One Flew Over the Cuckoo's Nest*, it presents the institution as an image of contemporary society – a paradigm of a world in which authority seeks to define reality, impose rules, coerce the individual, and in which the individual can respond only with a corrosive anarchy, for, as one of the play's central characters remarks, 'You can't be a rationalist in an irrational world. It isn't rational' (p. 428).

The play offers the by now familiar criticism of authority, with the Queen, Winston Churchill, the police and psychiatry being pilloried. But beyond its exuberant wit it does imply more substantial issues, the nature of the real, the desperate and ironic need to impose form on chaos, the inadequacy of the rational mind in a world not structured on rational principles. Unusual behaviour may indeed be the order of the day in a mental hospital, but the insanity with which Orton deals is not contained by the walls of an institution. It is a 'democratic lunacy'. Of course, farce has always sustained the notion that life is simply a game. The mistaken identities of French farce, the sexual taboos that are broken and the social etiquette that is momentarily abandoned are customary stages in a familiar and frivolous exercise. The indiscretions are themselves recognizable ploys in a game that will inevitably end with social roles happily reasserted, with broken relationships restored. But where such endings occur in Orton's work they are painfully ironic. Where Feydeau has flirtation, Orton has rape; where Feydeau has sexual misadventure, Orton has incest. In Feydeau sensibilities are offended, in Orton physical injuries are sustained. Feydeau's characters are driven to comic despair and momentary desperation, Orton's are driven to madness and death. Where Feydeau depends on the existence of a structured society, with its recognized codes and values, Orton presents a world in which normative values no longer exist, in which anarchy is the only dependable reality.

Indeed, the byzantine complexities of the plot of *What the Butler Saw* can be seen as a deliberate attempt to parody the very structure of farce itself. Mistaken identity is not so much a device as a way of life. Dr Prentice, a psychiatrist in a private clinic, attempts to seduce his new secretary, Geraldine, but is interrupted by the arrival of his wife, a member of a lesbian coven. Having successfully persuaded Geraldine to remove her clothes, he is now forced into a series of ever more desperate lies in order to conceal his attempted adultery. The complications increase as a hotel page, Nicholas Beckett, who has just seduced Prentice's wife in the linen closet of a nearby hotel, arrives on the scene, together with Dr Rance, a psychiatric government inspector, who attempts to make the increasingly bewildering events fit into the simple mould of his psychiatric theories. The two young outsiders are made to dress in one another's clothes in order to escape detection, a sexual confusion which causes even more trouble when a police sergeant appears on the scene. The consequent mayhem is abruptly resolved, after further complexities, when Geraldine and Nicholas are conveniently, if embarrassingly, revealed to be the twin offspring of a coupling between Prentice and his wife which had taken place years before in the much-used linen closet of the same hotel.

The play is close in spirit and to a degree in detail to *The Importance of Being Earnest*. The confusion of identity and the critique of solemnity and pomposity are indeed familiar enough. Each individual perceives a different reality and makes this the basis for actions which, while logical enough given the nature of the initial premiss, are irrational when viewed from any other perspective. And this is clearly proffered by Orton as an insight into human misunderstanding and the relativity of the physical and moral world. To some degree, of course, this would seem to be subverted by the privileged position granted to the audience, who believe themselves to be in possession of a perceivable truth, a reliable guide to the actual processes enacted in front of them. But this comfortable assurance, so necessary to the enjoyment of bourgeois farce, is destroyed at the end when they are made to see that what they took to be frivolous sexual games were in fact incestuous trysts in which a mother is raped by her son and a father attempts to strip and rape his daughter. The germ of moral anarchy is suddenly exposed at the centre of the conventional confection. And this is the essence of Orton's method.

Orton's consistent assault on authority, then, is both the gesture of a social rebel and an assertion of the contingent nature of the world we inhabit. His concern with the fragile boundaries of sexuality is not merely a defence of his own right to deviate from supposed norms but an assertion of everyone's right of dissent from all the principles and presumptions that form the basis of what we erroneously presume to be absolute standards of conduct and agreed codes of morality. His concern with the indefinable nature of reality, the fluid essence of identity and the relativity of truth constitutes a metaphysical as well as a social truth. It implies a conviction as to the antinomian nature of our universe; it is an assertion of the need to embrace uncertainty, the arbitrary, the neurotic, the kaleidoscopic fictions we create for ourselves. The authority he denounces is thus ultimately any kind of limiting or categorizing force, social or metaphysical, which is presumed to give shape and coherence to existence but which can do so only at the expense of the total freedom of action, that transgression of boundaries which is the only value he can identify. Dr Rance's claim that 'I am a representative of order, you of chaos' (p. 417) is ultimately a validation of anarchy, of self-invention, of the fictionalizing impulse.

4

COMEDY, FARCE AND THE SEXUAL IMAGE

The humour of Orton's work is not the moral agent that it conventionally is in much liberal literature. Malcolm Bradbury has pointed out, in the context of the reissue of his own 1950s novel *Eating People is Wrong*, that it evidences 'a more generous comedy than I would write now, in a world that has so changed'. For he recognizes that

> comedy has always been an essential aspect of the novel; it has something to do with its openness, its curiosity about people and society, and it administers precisely to that space between appearance and reality that has so long preoccupied English novelists.

This is, in fact, that comedy of reconciliation which Northrop Frye has called New Comedy. But he knows too that 'it also has had another vein, a vein of irony or absurdist farce, a sense of people at a loss in a totally contingent world.'[19]

It is this reification of comedy which has made Orton seem so central to modern preoccupations. It is, indeed, a shift from comedy to farce, since the moral world upon which comedy depends seems to many writers to have collapsed. Comedy becomes wedded to the grotesque. Dürrenmatt observes that 'Comedy alone is suitable for us. Our world has led us to the grotesque.'[20] But this is comedy pressed towards farce. The desolate landscapes of Beckett's world, the diminished social setting of Pinter's plays, the grotesque objectification of Ionesco's universe, themselves constitute a retreat from the comic into the farcical, for comedy depends upon a gap between inner self and mask which has collapsed. As one of

Mrozek's characters in *Tango* (translated by Tom Stoppard) suggests, 'Don't you see that nowadays tragedy isn't possible any more? . . . Today farce is the only thing possible.'[21] Orton pressed that conviction to its logical conclusion. It is in this sense that he became a pivotal figure, a crucial embodiment of the post-modernist impulse: by means of farce he gives expression to that conviction of a dislocated self, of a reified experience, of a brittle and contingent language, which still seems to define the nature of our private fears if not always of our public protestations.

Indeed, Orton was already claiming the centrality of farce as early as 1964, though it was hard to see how it related to *The Ruffian on the Stair*, the ostensible object of his remarks. Yet it was clear that, while that play was close in spirit to the ironic metaphysics of Harold Pinter, his emphasis lay not only on the comic but on deliberate provocation:

> If you weigh my play . . . in the balance of good taste you will find you have been short-measured. . . . Ten years ago this theme would have provided an addition to that moribund theatrical genre, Strong Drama. . . . Today it is farce.
>
> In a world run by fools the writer can only chronicle the doings of fools or their victims. And because the world is a cruel and heartless place, he will be accused of cruelty and heartlessness. If he thinks that the world is not [only] cruel and heartless but funny as well, he has given his critics an extra brickbat to fling and will be accused of not taking his subject seriously.
>
> But laughter is a serious business and comedy a weapon more dangerous than tragedy. Which is why tyrants treat it with caution. The actual material of tragedy is equally viable as comedy – unless you happen to be writing in English, when the question of taste occurs. The English are the most tasteless nation on earth, which is why they set such store by it.[22]

In a chapter on farce in his book *The Life of Drama* Eric Bentley draws attention to the Oedipal implications of comedy identified by Ludwig Jekels, a follower of Freud (who asserts that tragedy shows the son paying for his rebellion against the father, while comedy shows the son victorious and the father discomfited). Given Orton's obsessive concern with incest, this seems an apt observation. For Freud, jokes were of two basic types: they were either hostile (aggressive or satirical) or obscene (aimed at exposure), and their targets were reason, critical judgement and suppression. It is not hard to see the relevance of this to Orton, who worked through caricature, parody and travesty — modes which, Freud reminded us, are directed precisely 'against people and objects which lay claim to authority and respect'.[23]

Orton saw himself as living in a society and a time when it was no longer possible to believe that anomie could be solved by a simple shift in political objectives; that had been the particular illusion of the 1950s. He saw himself as inhabiting 'a very sick society' in which there was 'a general sense of despair about politics because we know it can't provide any real solutions.'[24] His response was to undermine it at first with absurdist comedy and then with farce, not in his mind an inherently inferior genre. By 1965 he was insisting that 'Farce is higher than comedy in that it is very close to tragedy.' In theory, he suggested, 'there is no subject which could not be treated farcically — just as the Greeks were prepared to treat any subject farcically. But in practice farce has become very restricted indeed.'[25]

Though in the latter part of his career he developed an intensely personal form of farce — brittle, contingent, violent and deliberately subversive of social and moral structures — his assumptions and comic techniques have their roots partly in the Restoration comedies he studied, partly in the verbal wit of Oscar Wilde, the satirical humour of Bernard Shaw and the mannered exoticisms of Ronald Firbank. If Restoration comedy was a licensed assault on a recently conquered Puritanism, Orton's anarchic farces were an attack on the stultifying morality of the fifties, itself already under fire. For Charles Lamb the achievement of Restoration comedy depended precisely on its exclusion of the moral ('a privation of moral light'[26]), an indifference generated by 'a chaotic people'. Its characters were essentially 'puppets'. This indifference is singled out as an essential element of humour by George Meredith ('indifference is its natural environment'[27]), while the notion of man as a kind of puppet is seen by Henri Bergson as a basic comic strategy ('we shall probably find that it [the work of comic artists] is generally comic in proportion to the clearness, as well as the subtleness, with which it enables us to see a man as a jointed puppet'[28]). Orton, who had claimed that prison 'brought detachment to my writing', and who asserted that as a consequence 'I wasn't involved any more',[29] not only relied on that indifference as method; he promoted it as a response. But, like Théophile Gautier, he recognized that the comic in its extreme form expresses the logic of the absurd. And, like Bergson, he seems to have felt that comedy conceals 'the beginnings of a curious pessimism'.[30] This was an observation echoed equally by Ionesco, who in 1964 observed that 'the tragic feeling of a play can be underlined by farce. . . . As the "comic" is an intuitive perception of the absurd, it seems to me more hopeless than the tragic.'[31]

Beckett's response to the absurd is to move towards minimalism and even silence; it is the generation of an austerity of style commensurate with a world that has excluded values too susceptible to irony to survive. His mode is to reduce without being reductive. It is as though his characters can hardly sustain protracted speeches. When they attempt more, the linguistic structure tends to collapse of its own weight, as it does in Lucky's speech in *Waiting for Godot*. Silence is the constant lure, apparently the only escape from irony, though itself, of course, the ultimate irony. For the most part Orton's approach seems wholly otherwise. His characters are not merely compulsive verbalizers, as some of Beckett's characters are; they are hyped on language. Particularly in the later plays, they leave none of the dangerous pauses and silences that characterize a Beckett or Pinter text. Language spills apparently carelessly, in a deluge of words. He was tempted by Beckett's strategy. He was attracted by figures like Congreve and Rimbaud who eventually chose silence. But it was an option that neither he nor his characters could claim. Throughout his brief life he wrote as compulsively as they spoke.

His is not a rich language, a language of substance and quality. On the contrary, it is a language consciously drained of moral force, of vitality and discrimination. It is hollow; if it resonates, it does so precisely as a result of the social, ethical and cultural void it barely conceals — a silence against which it strains, and which its hysterical excess ultimately defines. It is not a language generated by the characters themselves. They are merely puppets, mouthpieces; they aspire to the articulateness of their language, to the structured world of meaning and communication, but are repeatedly frustrated. The failure of aspiration to result in fulfilment is productive of absurdist farce as in another world it might have been productive of tragedy. *Head to Toe* concedes the force of language but launches its central character on a voyage towards silence. And this is a voyage to which all of his characters are condemned. Every joke, every *double entendre*, every unconscious witticism reveals the imprecision of language, its hopeless plasticity, its incorrigible arbitrariness, its undeniable irony, its ultimate emptiness. Its half-life is painfully short. It degrades between the thought and its expression.

Beckett's characters are imprisoned: in sand, in urns, dustbins, beds, chairs. They are already practically inanimate. They continue to live because they cannot abandon the hope that is one constituent of the absurdity from which they suffer and which they generate through their existence — like the writer himself, for whom 'There is nothing to express, nothing with which to express, nothing from which to express, together with an obligation to express.'[32] Orton's characters are free to move; indeed, in the later plays they do so in a state of frenzy. But it is a movement without direction, and they, too, are pulled towards the inanimate. Yet Orton exults in the freedom he denies his characters. Beckett confesses to being tied to the world whose ironies he dramatizes; Orton declares his independence, refuses to be coerced by an absurdity that depends on a lust for order which he derides. He submits to anarchy, which he sees as liberating him from a world of morality into one of aesthetics, from a destructive belief in a meaning that will not manifest itself, into a total contingency which he enacted in his private life and created in his public life.

If humour was to be an agent of degradation, if it was to expose contingency, to reveal the lying rationalism of language and the compulsion to deny the power of the inanimate, it also had another dimension. It could become an agent of social subversion, a flame to burn away inessentials, a mechanism to facilitate a protective detachment, a means of resisting a sense of order which potentially annihilated freedom. Inevitably, therefore, it also became a primary mechanism in destroying the apparent coherences of art itself, a principal device of Orton's antitheatre.

For Ionesco, *The Bald Prima Donna* was an antiplay because it offered a parody of a theatre that seemed to him to be essentially false. It was a similar logic that led Orton to farce. Like Ionesco he set out, in that playwright's words, to 'dismember the language' and to deride the standard concerns of the theatre, 'adultery, ideologies, politics – all sort of things which are not truly important or essential'.[33] Believing, with him, that 'all solutions are false, all engaged theatre is false', he too turned to the 'lucidity and liberty' of a humour that had the power to 'burst the crust'.[34] He too believed that 'You must arrive at a point where you can laugh at anything, as I must at the idea that I shall be a corpse', and believed that 'You must see things as they are and yet be detached from them', humour being a primary mechanism 'to achieve that detachment'.[35]

Orton's willed bad taste is thus less a calculated affront to decorum than a challenge to inertia and a deliberate assault on the notion of sanctity. His disgust with ossified versions of propriety is merely one aspect of his revolt against constraints of all kinds, against defining limits which privilege one activity over another, one form of sexuality over another – against, finally, death, the accoutrements of which are mocked in play after play.

Orton's humour, though in itself distinctive, is as strongly rooted in an English tradition as it is in classical Greek drama, the farce tradition of Europe and the absurdist disjunctions of Ionesco and Beckett. Thus, unsurprisingly, he was attracted to Oscar Wilde, whose sexuality and prison experience he shared and whose paradoxical humour he found compelling, eventually basing *What the Butler Saw* on *The Importance of Being Earnest*. The man who had written a poem to liberty celebrating the 'great Anarchies' which mirrored his wildest passions and gave 'my rage a brother'[36] was likely to prove attractive as a model. He admired Lewis Carroll for the logic of his bizarre imagination and in *Head to Toe* parodied a passage from *Alice in Wonderland*.[37] Like Ronald Firbank, whose work he read, he was drawn to a mannered wit and searched for humour in excess, in a displacement of the social and the psychological into the aesthetic, and in *Head to Toe* revealed the extent and nature of that influence, developing a prose style that seems to owe a great deal of its whimsicality, its admixture of the language of statecraft and fashion, to that author's *The Artificial Princess*. The Bernard Shaw that Orton admired was not the socialist writer of didactic comedies but the epigrammatist, the wry subversive. It is the Shaw who once observed that 'What is valid in Anarchism is that all Governments try to simplify their task by destroying liberty and glorifying authority in general and their own deeds in particular.'[38]

Thus, though Orton was appalled not merely by the procrustean reality of English society but also by an English sensibility that staunchly resisted a revivifying sensuality and a liberating anarchy of spirit, he drew deeply on a tradition of comic writing that had persistently done battle with this stultifying rigidity. He even employed as a basic strategy of his work a device that Henri Bergson had identified as a typical resource of comic writing in England: 'To express in reputable language some disreputable idea'[39] and likewise to transpose the solemn into the frivolous. Yet not the least remarkable aspect of Orton's brief career was the speed with which he shed his influences or incorporated them into a personal style which was so distinctive that it was hailed by writers as apparently diverse as Terence Rattigan and Harold Pinter.

*

Orton's stance seems to be essentially that proposed by Nietzsche in *The Birth of Tragedy*, which he summarized in 1886: 'I claimed that art, rather than ethics, constituted the essential metaphysical activity of man . . . that existence could be justified only in esthetic terms.'[40] For Sartre, aestheticism was a deliberate manœuvre of the bourgeoisie, who preferred to be denounced as philistines rather than as exploiters, but for Orton, as for Nietzsche, it was a conscious evasion of moralism. Morality, Nietzsche insisted, was 'a will to deny life, a secret instinct of destruction, a principle of calumny, a reductive agent . . . the Supreme Danger'. The counter-doctrine to what he called 'the Christian libel on life'[41] was contained in the form of Dionysus, the breaking of boundaries, participation in Dionysian revels, turning the individual from an artist into a work of art and inspiring an indifference towards the political instinct. This was essentially the path Orton followed, specifically identifying the Dionysian element in his work.

And sexuality, for both Nietzsche and Orton, was a primary agent of release. The Apollonian spirit emphasizes individuation and hence self-knowledge, rejecting excess and hubris; the Dionysian spirit represents sexual ambivalence and the extreme. There is little doubt where Orton would locate himself in such a debate and, when he used Euripides' *The Bacchae* as a distant model for *The Erpingham Camp*, he was celebrating a play in which Euripides was seemingly reacting against the Apollonian drive of his own career, conceding a victory of sorts to the disruptive power of Dionysus (though Orton was fully prepared to parody his technique and in particular the *deus ex machina* – a gesture towards utopianism that Orton would regard as nothing but ironic). For Nietzsche, tragic myth was 'Dionysian wisdom made concrete through Apollonian artifice'.[42] For Orton, this was equally a description of anarchic farce, and of his own artistic method. As he remarked,

I always say to myself that the theatre is the Temple of Dionysus, and not Apollo. You do the Dionysus thing on your typewriter, and then you allow a little Apollo in, just a little to shape and guide it along certain lines you may want to go along. But you can't allow Apollo in completely.[43]

In August 1964 Orton wrote a letter to Lindsay Anderson, offering a description of what would turn out to be *The Erpingham Camp* which makes plain the Dionysian thrust of his work:

This is the story of an eruption, an explosion, an outburst . . . of inspiration. . . . A representative group of sturdy, honest English folk, respectably pleasuring themselves at an August Holiday Camp, find themselves subjected to the influence of an intense, demonic leader. Their conventional habits – which anyway are more skin-deep than is generally supposed – are cast aside; they feel liberation; they abandon themselves under the tutelage of Don [Dionysus] to impulse.

66

. . . Propriety, in the person of the dubious Manager of the Camp, rashly attempts to intrude and to veto. But the forces of impulse are too strong; and catastrophe can be the only result . . .[44]

In Orton's work sexuality is aggression; it is subversion. It is a challenge to all authority, including, through his emphasis on incest, the authority of the parent, and, beyond that, perhaps of God, who is mocked not only in *Loot* and *Funeral Games*, but through a truculent rejection of all values except a total freedom of imagination and action. As Michel Foucault has suggested, 'the particular power of sexuality lies in the extent to which it operates as a challenge to language, to order, to limits.' For Orton, 'complete sexual licence [is] the only way to smash the wretched civilization. . . . Sex is the only way to infuriate them.'[45] It is principal; it is agent. In his own diary entries it is a curiously intransitive act; it is, as Foucault implies, a pursuit of some ultimate limit, a limit within rather than external to the self. Certainly Orton's sexual identity is crucial to his art. It was this in large part which established an unavoidable opposition between himself and the authorities empowered to control even this private aspect of his experience. But it went beyond this. Theodore Adorno has suggested that the common ground of Western moralists and ideologists of socialist realism is a hatred of sex. And plainly this was precisely the area of vulnerability that Orton chose to attack. English culture has always been susceptible to the writer who chooses to displace his politics from the political to the sexual sphere, as is evidenced by the gothic novel and the studied eroticism of the Romantic poets. A challenge to sexual norms is, after all, in part a challenge to normative values (viz. the American writers Charles Brockden Brown and Edgar Allan Poe or the English writers Emily Brontë and D. H. Lawrence). It was not for nothing that the Lord Chamberlain was charged with protecting English audiences from the sexually as well as the politically subversive. British politicians can survive accusations of financial speculation; detected in sexual indiscretion, they are consigned to the outer wilderness.

Orton replaced dialectics with excess. He sought the extreme as though to burn off the prosaic power of the real, the banalities of a bourgeois world for which he had complete contempt. He tried to make transgression itself a value, and in that process unregulated sexuality was an enabling strategy and a central fact rather than simply an image. Michel Foucault has observed that 'The twentieth century will undoubtedly have discovered the related categories of exhaustion, excess, the limit, and transgression – the strange and unyielding form of these irrevocable movements which consume and consummate us.' And central to this notion of transgression, to Foucault as to Orton, is sexuality, 'that firmament of indefinite unreality', which is 'tied to the still silent and groping apparition of a form of thought in which the interrogation of the limit replaces the search for totality and the act of transgression replaces the movement of contradictions.'[46] Dialectics are replaced by erotics; rational containment by irrational energy. Boundaries exist to be violated, and it is through such violations that meaning is generated.

George Steiner has argued that homosexuality tends to generate its own artistic strategies:

> From *art nouveau* to 'camp' and Gay Lib, homosexual codes and ideals are a major force. They seem to underlie, as if re-enacting their own solipsism, their own physiological and social enclosedness, that most characteristic of modern strategies: the poem whose real subject is the poem, art that is about self-possibility, ornament and architecture that have as their main referent not some grid of actual human use but other ornament or other form. So far as much of the best, of the most original in modern art and literature is autistic, i.e. unable or unwilling to look to a reality or 'normality' outside its own chosen rules, so far as much of the modern genius can be understood from the point of view of a sufficiently comprehensive, sophisticated theory of games, there is a radical homosexuality.[47]

Construed thus, the aesthetic of homosexuality becomes a rejection of realism as it is a revulsion from normative values. As a generalization such a comment is deeply suspect; in relation to Orton it is not without its relevance. A mannered hermeticism becomes a defence against the imperious demands of the real. Self-display becomes a protection against self-knowledge as well as from intrusion by the other. What chiefly typifies his characters is not that they wear masks which conceal a vulnerable humanity but that they exist only in and through that mask.

Orton's homosexuality gave him somewhere to stand outside the axial lines of social and psychological reality. Steiner goes even further, suggesting that homosexuality 'in part made possible that exercise in solipsism, that remorseless mockery of philistine common sense and bourgeois realism which is modern art.'[48] Homosexuality is thus seen by Steiner as an embrace of the self, its aesthetic correlative being a metatheatrical concern with process. And there is undeniably a hermetic quality to Orton's work: a private world closed off against ominous externalities. Incest (present in *Entertaining Mr Sloane* and *What the Butler Saw*) is an image of this closure, as it is in Faulkner's *The Sound and the Fury*. The play-acting, the camp style (a kind of Islington baroque), the provocations and the self-dramatizing are perhaps inextricably linked to his sexuality but so, too, are they to a period in which art's confidence in its own powers is under threat.

Orton mocks not only society but conventional narrative strategies and genres. He works through parody. As the formalist critic Sklovsky observed of Sterne's *Tristram Shandy*, it is this 'taking cognizance of form through violating it that constitutes the content'.[49] To a degree Orton was reminding us of the potential for subversion within farce. He was (to borrow another formalist observation) defamiliarizing a genre. Parody is, after all, an agent of release and of renovation. It is arguable – and indeed Theodore Adorno has argued precisely this – that in recent years politics has migrated into art that is apparently autonomous: that it exists most completely where it seems to be most carefully evacuated. Thus Kafka's novels or Beckett's plays are finally more subversive than many so-called committed works which 'by comparison . . . look like pantomimes', for

they explode from within the art which committed proclamation subjugates from without, and hence only in appearance. The inescapability of their work compels the change of attitude which committed works merely demand.

He over whom Kafka's wheels have passed, has lost for ever both any peace with the world and any chance of consoling himself with the judgement that the way of the world is bad; the element of ratification which lurks in resigned admission of the dominance of evil is burnt away.[50]

Seen thus, Orton becomes the ultimate critic inviting his audience to recuperate those values ruthlessly excluded from his plays.

*

In a sense, of course, he was himself destroyed by the forces of anarchy that he chose to embrace, for his lover's actions in beating his brains out and then destroying himself were consistent with the violent, reductive and morally irresponsible world that Orton created in his own work. His ignominious ending is curiously reminiscent of that which met Erpingham, or the characters in *The Ruffian on the Stair* or *Entertaining Mr Sloane*. It was an absurd and anticlimactic ending to his life which was entirely consistent with his work, a sudden and pointless ending close in spirit to that which he described in *Head to Toe*.

As he wanders the vast body of the dying giant, a Swiftian figure pursuing experience but learning nothing, Gombold Proval is systematically degraded and abused. Enrolled in a revolution, he finds himself in prison, his appeals for justice ignored, his gaol progressively more squalid. Conscripted to serve in a war between the left buttocks and the right buttocks, he ends up in a prisoner-of-war camp which doubles as a zoo, and there is classified as an ape and fed on scraps. Having escaped, he plunges down into the intestinal tract, continuing his journey until the giant himself sickens and dies. Whatever purpose might have been served by functioning as a louse in the body politic, a mite in a grand design beyond human understanding, is now destroyed as his whole universe begins to crumble, the apparent order and structure resolving into simple decay. The image is a familiar one. Mankind struggles to make sense of the marginal role it is required to play, desperately denying the evidence of its irrelevance to the implacable and elemental process of a decaying world. Man's need for order confronts an entropic reality, and out of that contradiction emerges the absurd. But Orton's protagonist chooses another response. Since he, and the universe in which he moves, is simply a product of his own imagination, he ends by climbing back into the darkness of his own fiction.

The book is as bitter as anything Orton ever wrote. It is an allegory of human life; it is also an account of his own fictive strategy. In a world in which INRI means nothing more than 'I Represent Idiots Now', in which 'Truth is relative, and always behind it stands some interest, furthering its own ends' (p. 69), the only possibility is to create 'a sort of seismic disturbance'. This is, indeed, how he saw his work. Yet, given his presumptions about the nature of human relations and the bleak world of daily unreality, he could place little faith in such an action. He was, he knew, like his own character in *Head to Toe*, a 'man who had a blackboard in his room on which he wrote with black chalk' (p. 69).

Indeed, in the filmscript he wrote for the Beatles, *Up Against It*, he took his anarchic and subversive tactics to an extreme. In a sequence developed from *Head to Toe*, but now recast as a vehicle for those other prototypical figures of the 1960s, he envisages a battle in which an ambulance collects the wounded only to crash in flames. The occupants are then collected by two other ambulances, and so on, until fleets of ambulances are on fire:

> At this point, with a loud roar, the earth caves in and the ambulances, full of suffering humanity, crash into the hole which has opened up in the treacherous subsoil. An army of stretcher bearers attempts to bring order to the scene. . . . Seeing what has happened before, they decline to be helped and fight off the stretcher bearers. . . . All this with the sound of rifle and Bren gun fire. Bells ringing. Trumpets sounding retreat. Shouts and screams from the injured. Blood pouring from bleeding wounds. On the edge of a gaping hole and the carnage of battle.

The image seems clear enough, and, when 'Onto the scene steps FATHER BRODIE, holding high the CROSS upon which OUR LORD died, accompanied by NUNS and CHOIR BOYS singing a hymn to the Glory of Immortal God',[51] the reductive irony could hardly be pressed further; hysteria, blasphemy, violence, absurdity, 'coils of sense and nonsense' melt and fuse 'into a vision'. The vision could scarcely be bleaker. The world he created, the life he lived, was stained with its humiliations and its violations. Treated with contempt by society, he responded in kind, eroding from within a system for which he had no respect, attacking the symbols of a sober authority which insisted on enforcing its models of order and of social and metaphysical meaning. In the circumstances, disorder, insanity, a careless proliferation of roles, was not, perhaps, without its homeopathic logic. Where Beckett responded to absurdity by shrinking his spacial, temporal and linguistic world to the point at which the ironies are attenuated, Orton drives his characters with a neurotic frenzy, fills the air with sound, hollows out language, implodes character and makes the ground literally collapse beneath their feet.

As Adorno implies, the temptation is perhaps to recuperate those values so patently absent from the plays, to respond to the crucial absences of the text, to see Orton's characters, as Adorno saw Beckett's, as 'what human beings have become', while 'the minimal promise of happiness they contain, which refuses to be traded for comfort, cannot be had for a price less than total dislocation, to the point of worldlessness.' But in truth Orton is less concerned with the generation of values than with ridiculing a world committed to the chimera of meaning. For him existence is less a matter of ethics than aesthetics, and accordingly, both in life and art, he developed a protean model of character; he created public personae and a series of characters that resisted the assaults of experience by pressing that experience to such extremes that it becomes simply parodic, merely aesthetic: life as a game, character as a kaleidoscope of roles, language as hopelessly plastic. And if this leaves him vulnerable to Adorno's observation that 'Formal structures which challenge the lying positivism of meaning can easily slide into a different sort of vacuity, positivistic arrangements, empty juggling with elements',[52] not the least of Orton's achievements lies in his refusal to succumb to this temptation. The mad, the chaotic, the subversive and the contingent have their victory in his work; the imagination reigns supreme. And this is the source of any redemptive force in his work – not the work itself, which is deliberately fragile, but the imagination that creates it.

The alarm at the amoral world Orton created was felt not only by the middle class, the philistine, the bluestocking. The association of literature and humanism was of long standing, and the argument over post-modernism's revulsion from the mimetic, its disregard for the moral, its concern with its own processes, continued through the 1970s and into the 1980s. For Christopher Lasch, the ironic detachment of such literature was no more than a response to the alienations of modern society. Faced with a stultifying routine, the individual

> seeks to escape from the resulting sense of inauthenticity by creating an ironic distance from his daily routine. He attempts to transform role playing into a symbolic elevation of daily life. He takes refuge in jokes, mockery and cynicism. . . . By refusing to take seriously the routines he has to perform he denies their capacity to injure him.[53]

By himself adopting a similar stance, by withdrawing from mimesis and the moral world, in Lasch's view the writer merely compounds those reifying forces and ties the individual and his society more securely to their fate.

There is, of course, something disturbing in the flight from reason, and Lasch is probably right to link it with the development of a form of narcissism. Certainly Orton's narcissism was undeniable; his callousness, raised to the dignity of willed indifference and ironic detachment, is as apparent in his diary entries as in his treatment of character. It could be argued that his apoliticism was an extreme form of politics, resignation being a means of confirming the status quo he affected to despise; and yet, as Lasch was prepared to concede, the power of contempt when directed at those in authority – the conscious withdrawal from complicity in the social process – may leave a vacuum that can be filled by more constructive forces than those that generated the cynicism in the first place.

When Lasch described the narcissistic personality he saw as typifying the seventies, he produced at the same time what was in effect a faithful portrait of Orton as he had been in the sixties, 'with his charm, his pseudo-awareness of his own condition, his promiscuous pansexuality, his fascination with oral sex, his fear of the castrating mother . . . his hypochondria, his protective shallowness, his avoidance of dependence, his inability to mourn, his dread of old age and death.'[54] But he was never simply this. For anarchy is not without its rights, and the deriding of those who seek order through imposing it is also a moral act. His plays did their work in exploding the solemnities of art no less than of society. The vision he projected offered no easy comfort. Like Beckett's characters, or, like his own protagonist Sloane, he acknowledged the desolation of the social and human environment. His art expressed this, but with its own frenetic energy it also opposed it. It is a familiar paradox, but one not without its dignity. For Robbe-Grillet, to invent the novel was to invent man. Orton might have said much the same of his theatre. His principal act of resistance is to reimagine the world, to deprive it of its power not merely by ridicule but by dislocating its language, destabilizing its models of behaviour, poisoning the wells of art, generating a sense of theatrical masks which contain the essence of the only available meaning and coherence. In the words of W. B. Yeats,

> If we cannot imagine ourselves as different from what we are and assume the second self, we cannot impose a discipline upon ourselves, though we may accept one from others. Active virtue, as distinct from the passive acceptance of a current code, is the wearing of a mask. It is the condition of an arduous full life.[55]

NOTES

1 Quoted in Malcolm Bradbury, *The Novel Today* (London, 1977), p. 7.
2 Alain Robbe-Grillet, *Snapshots and Towards a New Novel* (London, 1965), pp. 60, 63.
3 Quoted in James Fox, 'Joe Orton', *The Sunday Times Magazine*, 22 November 1970, p. 49.
4 Joe Orton, *Head to Toe* (London, 1971), pp. 148–9. All future references are incorporated into the text.
5 Nathanael West, *The Complete Works of Nathanael West* (London, 1957), p. 30.
6 Quoted in Christopher Butler, *After the Wake: An Essay on the Contemporary Avant-Garde* (Oxford, 1980), p. 135.
7 Harold Pinter, *The Room* (London, 1960), pp. 23–4.
8 Quoted in Butler, op. cit., p. 170.
9 Quoted in ibid., p. 20.
10 Sean O'Casey, *The Sean O'Casey Reader*, ed. Brooks Atkinson (London, 1968), p. 950.
11 Alain Robbe-Grillet, quoted in Butler, op. cit., p. 166.
12 Quoted in John Lahr, *Prick Up Your Ears: The Biography of Joe Orton* (London, 1978), p. 135.
13 C. G. Jung, *The Undiscovered Self*, trans. R. F. C. Hull (New York, 1958), pp. 21–2.
14 Quoted in Fox, op. cit., p. 52.
15 In Joseph F. McCrindle (ed.), *Behind the Scenes: Theatre and Film Interviews from the Transatlantic Review* (London, 1973), p. 118.
16 Erving Goffman, *The Presentation of Self in Everyday Life* (Harmondsworth, 1971), pp. 204–5.
17 Quoted in Max Schulz, *Black Humour Fiction of the Sixties* (Athens, 1973), p. 96.
18 Quoted in Fox, op. cit., p. 52.
19 Malcolm Bradbury, *Eating People is Wrong* (London, 1976), Introduction, p. 7.

20 Friedrich Dürrenmatt, 'Problems of the Theatre', in Robert W. Corrigan (ed.), *The Modern Theatre* (New York, 1965), p. 291.

21 Slawomit Mrozek, *Tango*, trans. Tom Stoppard (London, 1968), p. 64.

22 Quoted in Lahr, op. cit., p. 160.

23 Sigmund Freud, *The Standard Edition of the Complete Psychological Works of Sigmund Freud*, vol. 8 (London, 1960), p. 97.

24 Quoted in Lahr, op. cit., p. 166.

25 Ibid., pp. 225–6.

26 Charles Lamb, *The Life, Letters and Writings of Charles Lamb* (London, 1892), p. 365.

27 George Meredith, 'An Essay on Comedy', in Wylie Sypher (ed.), *Comedy* (New York, 1956), p. 63.

28 Henri Bergson, 'Laughter', in ibid., p. 80.

29 Quoted in Fox, op. cit., p. 49.

30 Bergson, op. cit., p. 189.

31 Eugène Ionesco, *Notes and Counter Notes*, trans. Donald Watson (New York, 1964), p. 27.

32 Samuel Beckett, *Three Dialogues with Georges Duthuit*, in *Proust and Three Dialogues* (London, 1970), p. 103.

33 Eugène Ionesco, 'Ionesco Talking', *Plays and Players* (April 1965), p. 50.

34 Ibid., p. 9.

35 Ibid., p. 50.

36 Oscar Wilde, *De Profundis and Other Writings* (Harmondsworth, 1976), p. 215.

37   'I expect you think this is a tree.'
       'As a matter of fact I don't. It's a hair.'
       'Whoever heard of a hair seventy feet long. You must be simple.'
       This remark was made in such an unpleasant tone that Gombold turned and walked away.
       'That path leads nowhere,' O'Scullion called as he plunged into the undergrowth.
       Gombold came back.
       'You might as well sit down.'
       'Which direction is best? . . .'
       'It depends upon where you want to get to,' he said closing his eyes.
       'I don't care.'
       'Then it doesn't matter which path you take.' (*Head to Toe*, p. 10)

38 Bernard Shaw, 'A Treatise on Parents and Children', in *Misalliance, The Dark Lady of the Sonnets, Fanny's First Play* (London, 1914), p. cxi.

39 Bergson, op. cit., p. 142.

40 Friedrich Nietzsche, *The Birth of Tragedy and the Genealogy of Morals*, trans. Francis Golffins (New York, 1956), p. 9.
41 Ibid., p. 11.
42 Ibid., p. 132.
43 Quoted in Lahr, op. cit., p. 15.
44 Ibid., p. 338.
45 Ibid., pp. 135–6.
46 Michel Foucault, *Language, Counter-Memory, Practice*, trans. Donald F. Bouchard and Sherry Simon (Oxford, 1977), pp. 49–50.
47 George Steiner, *On Difficulty and Other Essays* (Oxford, 1980), pp. 116–17.
48 Ibid., p. 118.
49 Quoted in Victor Erlich, *Russian Formalism* (New Haven, Conn., 1955; reissued 1981), p. 193.
50 Theodore Adorno, 'Commitment', in Ernst Block, Georg Lukács, Bertolt Brecht, Walter Benjamin, Theodore Adorno, *Aesthetics and Politics* (London, 1977), p. 191.
51 Joe Orton, *Up Against It* (London, 1979), pp. 61–2.
52 Adorno, op. cit., pp. 190–1.
53 Christopher Lasch, *The Culture of Narcissism* (New York, 1978), p. 95.
54 Ibid., p. 50.
55 Quoted in Ralph Ellison, *Shadow and Art* (New York, 1964), p. 53.

BIBLIOGRAPHY

WORKS BY JOE ORTON

Plays

Joe Orton: The Complete Plays, London: Eyre Methuen, 1976. New York: Grove Press, 1977.

Novel

Head to Toe. London: Blond, 1971.

Screenplay

Up Against It. London: Eyre Methuen, 1979. New York: Grove Press, 1979.

SELECTED CRITICISM OF JOE ORTON

Books

Lahr, John. *Prick Up Your Ears: The Biography of Joe Orton.* London: Allen Lane, 1978. Harmondsworth: Penguin, 1978. New York: A. A. Knopf, 1978.
McCrindle, Joseph F. *Behind the Scenes: Theatre and Film Interviews.* London: Pitman, 1973. New York: Holt, Rinehart & Winston, 1973.
Taylor, John Russell. *The Second Wave.* London: Methuen, 1971. New York: Hill & Wang, 1971.
Worth, Katherine. *Revolutions in Modern English Drama.* London: G. Bell, 1973.

Articles

Casmus, Mary I. 'Farce and Verbal Wit in the Plays of Joe Orton'. *Journal of Popular Culture*, 13 (1980), pp. 461–8.

Charney, Maurice. 'Occulted Discourse and Threatening Nonsense in Joe Orton's *Entertaining Mr Sloane*'. *New York Literary Forum*, 4 (1980), pp. 171–8.

Draudt, Manfred. 'Comic, Tragic, or Absurd? On Some Parallels Between the Farces of Joe Orton and Seventeenth Century Tragedy'. *English Studies*, 59 (1978), pp. 202–17.

Esslin, Martin. 'Joe Orton: The Comedy of (Ill) Manners'. In C. W. E. Bigsby (ed.), *Contemporary English Drama*. London: Arnold, 1981.

Fraser, Kenneth. 'Joe Orton: His Brief Career'. *Modern Drama*, 14 (1971), pp. 413–19.

Smith, Leslie. 'Democratic Lunacy: The Comedies of Joe Orton'. *Adam*, 40, 394–6 (1976), pp. 73–92.

Thompsen, Christian W. 'Joe Orton und das englische Theater der sechziger Jahre'. *Maske und Kothurn*, 19 (1973), pp. 321–41.